I0530126

The YOUTH BASEBALL Handbook

ALL-STAR EDITION

Learn the Basics, Improve Your Skills, and Develop Key Winning Strategies to Master the Game

Pathways Press

TABLE OF CONTENTS

INTRODUCTION

"Remember these two things: Play hard and have fun."
– Tony Gwynn

The moment a young player sets foot on the baseball field for the first time is a pivotal one—a blend of immense dreams and the palpable weight of the game's complexities. There's a unique mix of excitement and apprehension, a desire to hit the first home run yet a hesitation about where to begin. It's a scene that resonates deeply, not just with the young athletes but also with the coaches guiding them and the parents cheering from the sidelines. This shared sentiment forms the heart of our journey together through the pages of this book.

The purpose of "The Youth Baseball Handbook" is simple yet profound: to peel back the layers of baseball, transforming it from an intimidating maze into an exhilarating adventure of growth, skill enhancement, and a deeper love for the sport. This book is crafted to be your ultimate companion, whether you're a young player stepping up to bat, a parent navigating the nuances of youth sports, or a coach molding the next generation of athletes.

Our approach is holistic, transcending mere technical prowess. We delve into the mental and emotional facets of baseball, along with the strategic thinking that distinguishes good players from great ones. Through a tapestry of practical advice, motivational stories, and actionable strategies, we aim to guide every reader toward mastering the game.

At Pathways Press, we are driven by a mission to empower lives, and this handbook is a manifestation of that commitment. My personal journey through the world of youth baseball, marked by moments of triumph and learning, has fueled my passion to share this knowledge. It's a path I've walked both as a spectator on the sidelines and as an active participant in the sports community, experiencing firsthand the transformative power of youth sports.

As you navigate through this book, expect a journey that begins with the basics and gradually escalates to advanced strategies, without overlooking the crucial elements of mental resilience and the sheer joy of playing baseball. We've structured this guide to cater to all—whether you're just starting or seeking to refine your skills further, whether you're behind the bat or supporting from the stands.

Baseball is more than a game; it's a collective endeavor that binds teams, families, and coaches. This book aims to fortify these connections, fostering a supportive community united by a shared passion for the sport. It's about learning together, growing together, and perhaps most importantly, enjoying the journey together.

So, as we turn this page and step onto the field anew, let's do so with eagerness and an open mind, ready to embark on a transformative journey through the world of youth baseball. It's time to not just play, but to play better, guided by the insights and strategies within these pages. Together, let's turn dreams into reality, one inning at a time.

CHAPTER 1
UNDERSTANDING BASEBALL

"Baseball was, is, and always will be the best game in the world to me."
– Babe Ruth

On a bright, sunny afternoon, a field echoes with the crack of a baseball bat, a sound as deeply ingrained in American culture as the Star-Spangled Banner itself. This scene, familiar and cherished, serves not just as a pastime but as a thread in the fabric of history, weaving together generations. Baseball, more than a mere game, is a narrative of resilience, innovation, and unity. Its origins, iconic moments, legendary figures, and global impact offer a rich tapestry that mirrors societal changes and the unyielding spirit of competition and camaraderie.

1.1 THE HISTORY OF BASEBALL: A BRIEF OVERVIEW

Origins and Evolution

The roots of baseball stretch back to the 18th century, with various bat-and-ball games played in England. However, it was in the United States where baseball, as we recognize it today, truly began to form. Contrary to popular myth, Abner Doubleday did not invent baseball in Cooperstown, New York, in 1839. Rather, the game evolved from earlier versions like rounders and cricket. By the mid-19th century, amateur clubs like the New York Knickerbockers began to standardize rules, setting the stage for professional play. The National Association of Base Ball Players, formed in 1857, marked the game's first governing body, signaling baseball's burgeoning influence in American society.

Iconic Moments

Throughout its history, baseball has been punctuated by moments that have transcended the sport. Consider Jackie Robinson breaking Major League Baseball's color barrier in 1947, not just altering the game but advancing civil rights in America. Or Babe Ruth's called shot in the 1932 World Series, a legend blending bravado and skill. These moments and others—Hank Aaron surpassing Babe Ruth's home run record in 1974, Reggie Jackson's iconic 3 home run night in the 1977 World Series, and the Boston Red Sox reversing the Curse of the Bambino in 2004—have cemented baseball's role as a narrative vehicle for America's triumphs and challenges.

Baseball Legends

The saga of baseball is incomplete without its legendary figures, those whose prowess and personality have become folklore. Babe Ruth, with his larger-than-life persona and slugging records, set the benchmark for greatness. Jackie Robinson, whose courage and dignity under pressure paved the way for integration. Pitchers like Sandy Koufax and hitters like Ted Williams demonstrated the zenith of skill, while contemporaries like Derek Jeter and Ichiro Suzuki have carried the torch into the modern era. These athletes, among others, have not only defined excellence within the diamond but have also become cultural icons, embodying the values of perseverance, teamwork, and integrity.

The Global Game

Initially an American phenomenon, baseball has broadened its horizons, becoming a global game. The introduction of the World Baseball Classic in 2006 marked a significant milestone, bringing together national teams from around the world in a tournament that showcased the sport's international appeal. Baseball's inclusion in the Olympics, though intermittent, has furthered its reach, introducing the game to new audiences and fostering talent across continents. Countries like Japan, the Dominican Republic, and South Korea have become powerhouses, contributing to the diversity and richness of professional baseball in the United States and nurturing a shared global culture of baseball.

From its humble beginnings to its status as a cherished global sport, baseball offers a mirror to societal shifts and the enduring human spirit. Through each pitch, hit, and home run, the game continues to write its history, inviting players, enthusiasts, and casual observers alike to be part of its unfolding story.

1.2 UNDERSTANDING BASEBALL: TERMS AND LINGO

In the vibrant world of baseball, a unique language thrives—one that encapsulates the essence of the game, its strategies, and the camaraderie among its players and fans. This linguistic tapestry not only enriches the experience of the game but also serves as a bridge connecting newcomers to the deep traditions and nuances of baseball. Grasping this lingo is akin to learning the secret handshake of an exclusive club, offering insight into the game's heart and soul.

Basic Terminology

- Ball: A pitch that lands outside the strike zone, which the batter does not swing at. Four balls grant the batter a walk to first base.

- Strike: A term with a dual meaning; it refers to a pitch within the strike zone that the batter fails to hit or a swing by the batter that misses any pitch. Three strikes result in a strikeout.

- Run: The lifeblood of the game's score, a run is tallied each time a player successfully rounds all the bases and touches home plate.

- Out: A fundamental defensive goal, an out is recorded in numerous ways, such as when a batter strikes out, a fielder catches a hit ball before it touches the ground, or a runner is tagged before reaching a base.

Position Names and Numbers

In the choreography of baseball, each player on the field assumes a role that is pivotal to the team's defense, identified not just by names but by numbers—a system that streamlines communication and analysis.

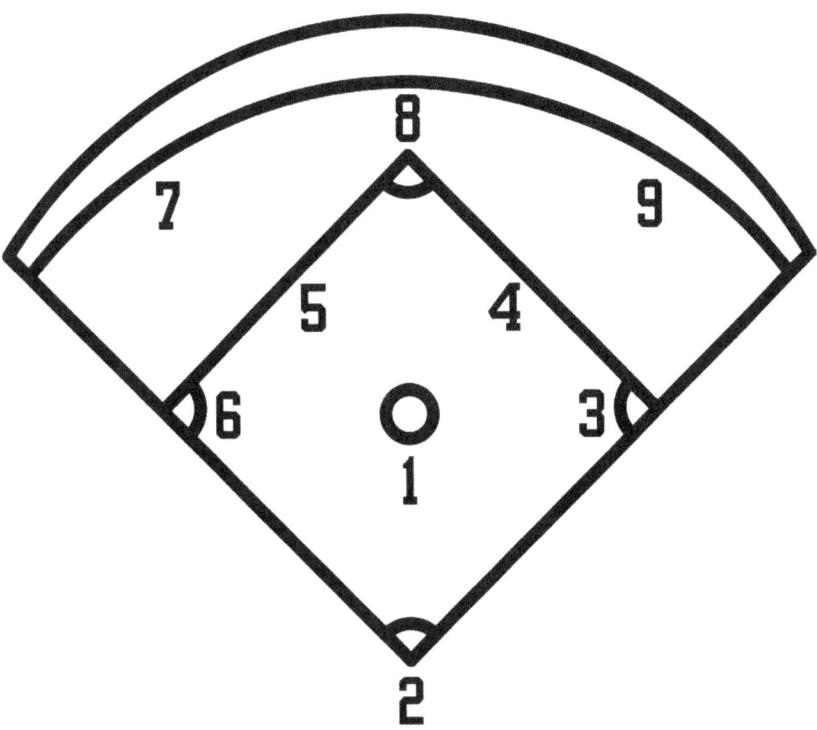

1. Pitcher (1): The maestro of the game, dictating its pace with every pitch.
2. Catcher (2): The strategist behind home plate, guiding pitchers and guarding the path to runs.
3. First Baseman (3): The guardian of first base, adept at catching throws and tagging runners.
4. Second Baseman (4): A versatile player who covers the area between second and first, key in double plays.

5. Third Baseman (5): Positioned by third base, often receives hard-hit ground balls and is crucial in stopping runners from scoring.

6. Shortstop (6): Occupies the gap between second and third bases, a linchpin in the infield defense.

7. Left Fielder (7): Covers the left segment of the outfield, backing up the infield and preventing base hits from evolving into extra bases.

8. Center Fielder (8): With a territory spanning the middle of the outfield, demands speed and an excellent arm.

9. Right Fielder (9): Guards the right portion of the outfield, often with a strong arm to throw far distances.

Common Slang and Expressions

Baseball's vernacular is as colorful as its history, with slang that adds flavor to its narratives.

- "Can of Corn": An easy-to-catch fly ball, as simple as grabbing a can off a grocery shelf.
- "In the Hole": The batter next in line after the on-deck hitter, preparing mentally for their turn.
- "Painting the Corners": A pitcher's skill in throwing strikes close to the edges of the strike zone.
- "Touch 'em All": A call to action for a player who has hit a home run to round all bases and score.
- "Bush League": Describes unprofessional conduct or minor-league play, often used to critique a lack of sportsmanship.

Scoring and Stats

In baseball, every run, hit, and out is a story, etched into the game's statistics—a numerical diary of triumphs, trials, and the relentless pursuit of excellence.

- Runs Batted In (RBI): Celebrates a player's effectiveness in generating runs, counting the number of times a batter enables a teammate to score.
- Batting Average (BA): A measure of a hitter's performance, calculated by dividing hits by at-bats, offering insight into consistency and skill.
- Earned Run Average (ERA): Quantifies a pitcher's reliability, averaging the number of earned runs allowed per nine innings, with a lower ERA signifying superior pitching.
- Fielding Percentage: Reflects a player's defensive prowess, determined by the ratio of putouts and assists to total chances, highlighting precision and agility in the field.

In the unfolding of a baseball game, every pitch, swing, and catch is a dialogue, narrated through this rich lexicon and the myriad statistics that map the game's ebb and flow. For enthusiasts, players, and scholars of the game, this language is not just a means of communication but a lexicon of passion, a testament to baseball's enduring allure and its capacity to unite across the expanse of fields, generations, and cultures.

1.3 THE SIGNIFICANCE OF
TEAM SPORTS IN YOUTH DEVELOPMENT

Team sports, with baseball at the forefront, play a pivotal role in shaping young minds and bodies. Through the dynamic interplay of competition and collaboration, baseball offers a fertile ground for nurturing a spectrum of vital skills and values, from social interaction and physical health to mental resilience and life lessons that transcend the diamond.

Social Skills

In the heart of baseball lies the essence of teamwork. Every pass, every base covered, and every strategy discussed in the dugout weaves a thread of camaraderie among players. It's here, amidst the cheers and high-fives, that young athletes learn the art of communication. Clear, concise exchanges between the pitcher and catcher, the infielders calling out plays, and outfielders signaling to one another exemplify the critical importance of verbal and non-verbal communication. Beyond this, leadership emerges naturally on the field. Players often rotate leadership roles, sometimes leading by example through a crucial play or by rallying the team in the face of adversity, teaching them the value of stepping up when the team needs direction and support.

Physical Health

The physical benefits of engaging in baseball are extensive and impactful. From sprinting to bases and chasing down fly balls to the explosive power needed for batting and the agility required for fielding, baseball hones the body's coordination and fitness levels. Regular participation helps build muscle strength, especially in the arms, legs, and core, and enhances cardiovascular health through the bursts of running involved in the game. Moreover, the diverse range of movements in baseball, from sliding to catch a low ball to leaping for a high one, improves flexibility and general body coordination, laying a foundation for a lifetime of physical activity and health.

Mental Benefits

Baseball also serves as a powerful tool for mental and emotional development. The structure and routine of regular practices and games offer a reassuring stability, contributing to stress relief by providing an outlet for energy and anxiety. Success on the field, whether a well-hit ball, a strikeout, or a game won, boosts self-esteem and confidence, affirming the player's capabilities and hard work. Furthermore, the game teaches focus and concentration, as players must stay mentally engaged to anticipate and react to the fast-paced developments of each inning. This heightened state of mental alertness and the satisfaction derived from mastering new skills or contributing to a team's victory nurture a sense of fulfillment and joy, crucial components of mental well-being.

Life Lessons

Perhaps most significantly, baseball is a rich source of life lessons that mold young players into resilient, disciplined, and empathetic individuals. Discipline is cultivated through the rigorous training and adherence to the rules of the game, teaching players the value of commitment and hard work. Perseverance is another critical lesson learned on the field; baseball, with its inherent ups and downs, teaches young athletes to keep striving, regardless of the score or situation. It instills in them an understanding that setbacks are temporary and that determination and effort can turn the tide.

Moreover, baseball teaches young players how to deal with failure—a skill as vital off the field as it is on it. Striking out or missing a catch is part of the game, offering teachable moments on handling disappointment, learning from mistakes, and bouncing back stronger. These experiences foster resilience, enabling players to face life's challenges with grit and grace. Equally important, baseball promotes empathy and sportsmanship. Players learn to respect their opponents, appreciate the efforts of their teammates, and understand the value of fair play, nurturing a sense of fairness and empathy that extends beyond the game.

In the microcosm of a baseball game, young players experience a condensed version of life's broader lessons. The field becomes a classroom where teamwork, communication, leadership, discipline, perseverance, and empathy are taught through every inning played. These lessons, woven into the fabric of their development, equip young athletes with the skills and values needed to navigate the complexities of life with confidence and integrity.

1.4 BASEBALL EQUIPMENT 101: WHAT EVERY BEGINNER NEEDS

Before a player can step onto the field and feel the thrill of hitting a ball or making a catch, they need the right tools for the job. The gear a player uses is not just about looking the part; it's about safety, comfort, and enhancing performance. Here, we'll break down the basics of what gear is needed to get started in baseball, how to choose it wisely, and keep it in top condition.

Essential Gear

- Gloves: A good glove is like a best friend to a baseball player; it's essential for catching and fielding. Players in different positions might need specific types of gloves. For example, catchers use a mitt with extra padding to handle fast pitches, while infielders prefer gloves with a shallow pocket for quick ball retrieval.
- Bats: Bats can vary significantly in size, weight, and material. While metal bats are common in youth leagues for their durability and enhanced power, learning the nuances of using a wooden bat can also be beneficial for developing a good hitting technique.
- Helmets: Safety first. A helmet protects the batter's head from fast pitches. It's crucial for it to fit snugly and be in good condition, without cracks or significant wear.
- Baseballs: Practice balls may differ from game balls, but it's important to have a good supply for training. Look for balls that are appropriate for the player's league and age group.

- Cleats: Good traction is important for running, batting, and fielding. Baseball cleats come designed specifically for the sport's movements, with options available for different field types like grass or turf.
- Protective Gear: This includes catchers' gear, batting gloves, and elbow or shin guards. Each piece serves to protect players from injuries during the game's various aspects, from catching to batting.

Choosing the Right Equipment

Selecting baseball gear can be overwhelming with so many options. However, focusing on fit and comfort can guide decisions. For gloves, the hand should feel snug but not tight, with enough flexibility to open and close the glove easily. When choosing a bat, the player should be able to swing it comfortably without straining; a general rule is to select the heaviest bat that can be swung with speed. Helmets should fit tightly without wobbling, and cleats should offer support and comfort without causing blisters. It's also wise to consult with coaches or experienced players, as they can offer valuable advice tailored to the player's needs and position.

Maintenance and Care

Taking care of baseball equipment not only extends its life but also ensures it performs well. Gloves should be regularly conditioned with glove oil to keep the leather soft and prevent cracking. Bats, especially wooden ones, may need occasional sanding or treatment with bat wax to maintain their surface.

Helmets, cleats, and protective gear should be inspected regularly for signs of wear and tear, and cleaned according to manufacturer instructions to maintain their protective qualities. Storing equipment properly is also key; keeping it in a cool, dry place away from direct sunlight helps prevent damage.

Safety Considerations

The right gear does more than improve a player's game; it's a crucial line of defense against injuries. Helmets are a must at all times for batters, base runners, and catchers, significantly reducing the risk of head injuries. Catchers should wear full protective gear, including a mask, chest protector, and shin guards, to safeguard against fast pitches and foul balls. Using batting gloves can help prevent blisters and absorb shock, reducing hand fatigue and the risk of dropping the bat. For all players, wearing a protective cup is advised for additional safety. Above all, ensuring that all equipment is well-fitted and in good condition is fundamental to preventing injuries on the field.

The equipment a player brings to the field is more than just gear; it's their armor and toolkit, essential for playing safely and at their best. From the glove that snags a high fly ball to the cleats that grip the dirt on a sprint to first base, each piece plays a role in the unfolding drama of a baseball game. Taking the time to select the right equipment, care for it properly, and wear it consistently ensures that players can focus on what they love most about the game: the joy of play, the thrill of competition, and the camaraderie of the team.

1.5 THE ROLE OF PARENTS AND COACHES: BUILDING SUPPORTIVE ENVIRONMENTS

In the tapestry of youth baseball, parents and coaches hold the threads that can either weave a supportive environment or unravel the fabric of a young player's enthusiasm. Their influence extends far beyond the field, shaping the player's attitude towards the game, their teammates, and themselves.

Creating a Positive Atmosphere

The atmosphere surrounding young athletes can significantly impact their performance and enjoyment of the game. A positive, nurturing environment encourages players to take risks, learn from their mistakes, and push their boundaries without fear of retribution or disappointment. Both parents and coaches play critical roles in cultivating this atmosphere. They should celebrate efforts, not just outcomes, and focus on the joys of playing rather than the pressures of winning. A simple yet impactful practice is to highlight the positives after a game, acknowledging areas of improvement while reinforcing the player's strengths and contributions.

Balancing Competition and Fun

Baseball, at its core, is a game meant to be enjoyed. While competition can drive excellence, an overemphasis on winning can diminish the fun, leading to burnout and loss of interest. Striking a balance between competitive play and enjoyment is crucial. Coaches can infuse practices with a variety of activities that foster skill development while keeping the mood light and engaging. Scrimmages, skill challenges, and baseball-related games can break the monotony of routine drills, keeping players excited about coming to practice. Parents can support this balance by prioritizing fun over performance in discussions about the game, encouraging play for the sake of enjoyment rather than the pressure of achievement.

Communication with Young Athletes

Effective communication forms the backbone of any successful team and player development strategy. It's about more than conveying information; it's about connecting, understanding, and guiding young athletes. Coaches can adopt an open-door policy, encouraging players to share their thoughts, concerns, and goals. This approach not only fosters a strong coach-player relationship but also provides valuable insights into how best to support each player's development. Parents, on their part, can maintain open lines of communication with their children, listening actively to their experiences and feelings about the game. This includes discussing their challenges and triumphs, offering a listening ear rather than immediate advice or judgment. Such conversations can reinforce the child's self-esteem and motivation.

- Ask open-ended questions: Encourage players to express themselves fully, avoiding yes or no answers. Questions like "What was your favorite part of today's game?" or "How did you feel about your performance at bat today?" prompt reflection and discussion.

- Provide constructive feedback: Focus on specific, actionable feedback that players can use to improve. Highlight what they did well and offer suggestions for areas of improvement.
- Celebrate effort over outcome: Recognize and praise the effort, dedication, and improvement, showing that these are valued over winning or stats.

Encouraging Growth and Learning

At the heart of youth sports lies the opportunity for personal growth and learning. Baseball offers myriad lessons in resilience, teamwork, discipline, and sportsmanship. Parents and coaches can encourage this growth by setting realistic goals, celebrating small victories, and viewing mistakes as learning opportunities rather than failures. This approach helps young athletes develop a growth mindset, where challenges are seen as chances to improve rather than insurmountable obstacles. Encouraging players to set personal goals, aside from team objectives, allows them to focus on individual progress and find personal success within the team's framework.

- Set achievable goals: Work with players to set realistic, attainable goals that motivate them to improve. These could be skill-based, like mastering a new pitch, or behavioral, like showing better sportsmanship.
- Focus on progress: Highlight how far the player has come from the start of the season, acknowledging growth and improvement to motivate continued effort.

- Use mistakes as teachable moments: Instead of dwelling on errors, discuss what can be learned from them. This might involve reviewing a play to identify decision-making opportunities or practicing a skill to correct a technical mistake.

In every cheer, every piece of advice, and every moment spent practicing and playing, parents and coaches have the power to shape a young player's experience of baseball. It's a responsibility that goes beyond teaching the rules of the game or techniques of play. It's about nurturing a love for the game, respect for oneself and others, and the joy of playing for the sake of playing. Through their actions, words, and attitudes, parents and coaches can create an environment where young athletes thrive, not just in baseball but in life.

1.6 SETTING REALISTIC GOALS: THE FIRST STEP TO SUCCESS

In the world of youth baseball, the setting of goals is the cornerstone upon which success is built. It's not just about aiming to win games; it's about laying down a path of personal and team growth that leads to a deeper understanding and love for the game. The art of setting goals that are both challenging and achievable is a skill in itself, one that players, coaches, and parents can develop together.

Individual Goals

For young players, personal goals provide a framework for improvement that is uniquely theirs. It starts with identifying areas of their game they're passionate about or feel need enhancement. A player might aim to improve their batting average, develop a new pitch, or increase their base-stealing speed. The key is to ensure these objectives are specific enough to be measurable and realistic enough to be achievable within a given timeframe.

- Skill Improvement: Players should identify specific skills they wish to improve, such as batting technique or fielding precision. Setting quantifiable benchmarks, like achieving a certain batting average or reducing errors, makes progress tangible.

- Enjoyment of the Game: Goals need not be solely performance-related. Young athletes should also set goals around their enjoyment of the sport, such as trying new positions, making new friends on the team, or simply learning to appreciate the game's subtleties.

Team Objectives

While baseball has individual aspects, it is fundamentally a team sport. Setting team goals can help build a sense of unity and shared purpose, which is crucial for a successful season. These goals might range from improving the team's overall win-loss record to developing a reputation for excellent sportsmanship or becoming known for a never-give-up attitude. Coaches play a vital role here, guiding the team in setting objectives that inspire and challenge, while also fostering an environment where every player feels valued and integral to the team's success.

- Unity and Purpose: Goals such as improving team communication, supporting each other through wins and losses, and working together to overcome challenges can strengthen the bonds between players.

- Collective Improvement: Objectives that focus on collective skill development, such as executing specific plays with precision or improving team batting averages, encourage players to support each other's growth.

Measuring Progress

Tracking progress towards goals is essential for maintaining motivation and adjusting strategies as needed. For individual goals, players might keep a journal or log of their performance in games and practices, noting improvements, challenges, and the strategies that helped them succeed. For team goals, regular check-ins during practice sessions can help assess how well the team is working towards its objectives, celebrating successes and identifying areas for further effort.

- Effort Over Outcomes: While outcomes are important, emphasizing effort and improvement can help young players stay motivated and focused on growth, regardless of immediate results.
- Regular Review: Setting aside time for regular review of progress, both individually and as a team, ensures goals remain front and center, adjusting approaches as necessary.

Adjusting Goals

Flexibility is crucial in the goal-setting process. As players grow and evolve, so too should their goals. A player might master a skill more quickly than anticipated, necessitating a new challenge, or they might encounter unexpected difficulties, requiring a reassessment of their objectives. Similarly, team goals might shift in response to changes in team dynamics, achievements, or challenges faced during the season.

- Growth and Challenges: Recognizing when a goal has been met or when it no longer serves its purpose allows players and teams to remain engaged and challenged.
- Changing Interests: As young players explore the multifaceted world of baseball, their interests may shift. Goals should be adaptable to accommodate changing passions, ensuring the sport remains enjoyable and rewarding.

In essence, the journey through a baseball season, marked by the pursuit of carefully chosen and meaningful goals, offers young players, their teammates, and coaches a structured yet flexible framework within which to grow, learn, and celebrate the game. This approach not only enhances performance on the field but also enriches the experience of baseball, making it a powerful vehicle for personal development and team cohesion. Through setting and striving towards individual and team goals, the youth baseball experience becomes not just about hits, runs, and outs, but about cultivating discipline, teamwork, resilience, and a lifelong love for the game.

1.7 THE BASICS OF BASEBALL RULES: A GUIDE FOR NEW PLAYERS AND FANS

Baseball, with its blend of strategy and skill, captivates hearts with a rulebook that has evolved yet preserved the essence of the game over centuries. Understanding these rules not only enriches the viewing experience but also lays a solid foundation for players at all levels.

Game Structure

The structure of a baseball game is both simple and intricate, inviting players and spectators into a rhythmic dance of innings, outs, and the dynamic roles of offense and defense. A standard game unfolds over nine innings, with each inning divided into two halves. In the top half, the visiting team bats, striving to score runs, while the home team defends the field. The roles switch in the bottom half. The team with the most runs at the game's conclusion emerges victorious. Each team aims to secure three outs to end the opposing team's turn at bat, utilizing a combination of pitching prowess and defensive strategy.

- The pitcher faces each batter, aiming to secure strikes that lead to outs.
- Fielders strategically position themselves to catch hits or tag runners, aiming to halt the offense's advance.
- The batting team sends players in a predefined order to hit and run bases, accumulating runs.

Key Rules

At the heart of baseball's intrigue are its rules, which govern the game's flow and strategy.

- Strike Zone: A conceptual box over home plate between the batter's knees and the midpoint of their torso. A pitch within this zone, not swung at, is a strike; outside pitches are balls unless swung at.

- Base Running Rules: Runners must touch each base in order and can be tagged out if caught off base by the ball. Stealing bases, or advancing before the ball is hit, adds a thrilling layer of strategy.

- Scoring: Runs are scored when a player successfully rounds all bases and returns to home plate. A home run, where the ball is hit out of the field, allows the hitter and any players on base to score unchallenged.

- Forced Out: Occurs when a runner must advance to the next base to make room for a following runner, making them vulnerable to being out if the ball reaches the base first.

Penalties and Violations

Understanding penalties and violations clarifies why certain plays unfold as they do, adding depth to the game's strategy.

- Balk: A pitcher's illegal motion deceiving a base runner, resulting in all runners advancing one base.

- Interference: When a player unlawfully obstructs an opponent, potentially resulting in outs or base advancements, depending on the situation.

- Foul Balls: Hits that land outside the field's fair lines. They count as strikes unless the batter already has two strikes.
- Errors: Mistakes by fielders that allow batters or runners to advance. While not a formal penalty against the team, errors can lead to unearned runs and impact a player's statistics.

Unique Aspects

Baseball's ruleset includes several unique aspects that contribute to its unpredictability and excitement.

- The Infield Fly Rule: To prevent fielders from taking advantage of pop flies that could easily be caught for outs, any fly ball that can be caught by an infielder with ordinary effort, when there are runners on first and second (or the bases are loaded) with less than two outs, is automatically an out.
- The Designated Hitter (DH): Used primarily in the American League, the DH bats in place of the pitcher, adding strategic depth to lineup construction and in-game management.
- The Double Switch: A strategy in the National League where a manager substitutes a player in the lineup and simultaneously switches their position with another player to optimize batting order and pitcher replacement strategy.
- The Tag-Up Rule: Allows players to advance bases on a caught fly ball, provided they "tag up" or touch the base they occupied after the catch is made, creating moments of daring strategy and split-second decisions.

In the weave of baseball's rules, every pitch, swing, and sprint carries the weight of strategy, skill, and the centuries-old love for the game. For new players and fans, peeling back the layers of this rulebook reveals not just the mechanics of play but the heart of baseball itself—a game of precision, strategy, and endless possibilities. Each rule, from the path of a pitch to the sprint for home plate, is a thread in the larger tapestry of the game, connecting past to present and player to fan in the shared language of baseball.

1.8 THE IMPORTANCE OF SPORTSMANSHIP IN BASEBALL

In the heat of competition, where emotions run high and the desire to win can overshadow everything else, sportsmanship stands as the guiding principle that ensures baseball remains a game of respect, integrity, and camaraderie. This unwavering respect for all participants, the gracious acceptance of outcomes, and the collective effort to foster a positive environment are the cornerstones of true sportsmanship in baseball.

Respect for Players and Officials

At its core, baseball, like all sports, is built on mutual respect—respect not only for the game's rules but for everyone who steps onto the field. This includes teammates who share the highs and lows of the season, opponents who push each other to excel, and umpires who ensure the game's integrity. Young players learn early on that cheering for a teammate's success, acknowledging an opponent's skill with a tip of the cap, or accepting an umpire's call without protest are acts that elevate the game. This respect is crucial, as it teaches players to value effort and integrity over simply winning or losing.

- Positive Reinforcement: Coaches and parents should recognize and praise acts of sportsmanship, reinforcing that respect is as valuable as any on-field achievement.
- Role Modeling: Demonstrating respect in their interactions, adults show young players how to treat others with dignity, teaching through action that respect is a fundamental aspect of the game.

Handling Victory and Defeat

How young players handle the outcomes of games—be it a win that had the crowd on its feet or a loss that was hard to swallow—shapes their character both on and off the field. Learning to accept victory with humility and defeat with dignity is essential. Celebrating a win should never involve demeaning the losing team; instead, it's an opportunity to acknowledge the effort of all players. Similarly, facing a loss isn't about assigning blame but about recognizing the opponent's skill and understanding what can be improved for next time.

- Reflection After Games: Encourage players to reflect on their performance and the game's outcome, focusing on what was learned rather than the final score.
- Emphasizing Improvement: Shift the conversation from winning or losing to improvement and growth, helping players understand that both outcomes offer opportunities to learn.

Role of Parents and Coaches in Modeling Behavior

The behavior of adults—parents and coaches alike—sets the tone for young players' attitudes towards sportsmanship. When adults display respect for officials, empathy for players of both teams, and a focus on the joy of the game rather than the outcome, they model the behaviors they wish to see in young athletes. Negative sideline behavior or criticism of officials teaches the opposite, undermining the values of sportsmanship and respect. By embodying the principles of good sportsmanship, adults can significantly influence young players to do the same.

- Constructive Feedback: Instead of criticizing, offer constructive feedback that helps young players see setbacks as opportunities for growth.
- Supportive Sidelines: Parents and coaches should lead by example, showing respect for all players and officials from the sidelines, emphasizing encouragement over criticism.

Building a Positive Team Culture

A team's culture can significantly impact young players' experience of the game, influencing not just their performance but their enjoyment and personal growth. A culture that prioritizes sportsmanship, mutual respect, and support creates an environment where players feel valued and motivated. This involves setting clear expectations for behavior, celebrating acts of sportsmanship, and fostering a sense of unity and shared purpose among the team.

- Team Meetings: Regular team meetings can reinforce the values of sportsmanship, allowing players to share experiences and discuss the importance of respect and support.
- Team Building Activities: Activities outside of regular practices and games can strengthen bonds between players, encouraging a sense of brotherhood and mutual respect that carries onto the field.

In the world of youth baseball, sportsmanship is the golden thread that binds the game's many facets together. It is the principle that ensures baseball remains a vehicle for teaching life's most valuable lessons—respect for oneself and others, the grace to accept outcomes, and the integrity to play the game with honor. Through every pitch, hit, and catch, the true spirit of baseball shines brightest not in the scoreboard but in the moments of sportsmanship that define the character of young players, guiding them to become not just better athletes but better individuals.

1.9 NAVIGATING YOUR FIRST BASEBALL SEASON

Entering the world of baseball, especially for young players experiencing their debut season, comes with its own set of anticipations and uncertainties. The initial foray into this sport is not just about acquiring new skills but also about understanding the ethos of teamwork, the thrill of competition, and the personal growth that comes from both.

Preparation Tips

Getting ready for the first season requires a mix of physical readiness, mental preparation, and a basic grasp of the game's rules and strategies.

- Physical Conditioning: Start with exercises that enhance overall fitness—running for cardiovascular health, plyometrics for explosiveness, and basic strength training focusing on the core, legs, and arms. Incorporating baseball-specific drills, like catching, throwing, and batting practice, helps refine skills and builds muscle memory.

- Mental Preparation: Familiarize yourself with the game's rules and positions. Watching games, whether live or recorded, can also provide insight into gameplay and strategies. Visualization techniques, where players imagine themselves succeeding in various game situations, can boost confidence and reduce anxiety.

- Learning the Rules: Understanding the basics—from strike zones to the significance of different pitches—provides a solid foundation. Interactive quizzes or games focused on baseball rules can make this learning process engaging.

What to Expect

Setting realistic expectations for the first season can help temper nerves and build resilience against inevitable setbacks.

- Embrace Challenges: Recognize that mistakes are part of the learning process. Whether it's missing a catch or striking out, each misstep is an opportunity for growth.

- Celebrate Small Victories: Acknowledge personal achievements, no matter how minor they might seem. A successful hit, a well-fielded ball, or simply overcoming nervousness to play can all boost confidence.
- Understand Team Dynamics: Team sports involve navigating various personalities and roles. Not every interaction will be smooth, but learning to work as part of a team is a valuable life skill.
- Enjoy the Experience: Remember, the primary goal is to enjoy the game. Winning is exciting, but the joy of playing, the camaraderie among teammates, and the personal satisfaction of improvement are equally important.

Building Relationships

The bonds formed with teammates and coaches are integral to the baseball experience. These relationships can provide support during challenging times, enhance the joy of successes, and contribute to personal and athletic growth.

- Engage with Teammates: Take the initiative to know your teammates. Simple gestures like cheering for others' successes, offering encouragement, or sharing a laugh can foster a positive team environment.
- Communicate with Coaches: Coaches are not just instructors but mentors. Asking for feedback, seeking advice on areas of improvement, or discussing any concerns can help build a trusting relationship. Remember, coaches want to see players succeed, both on and off the field.

- Participate in Team Activities: Many teams organize activities outside of regular practices and games. These can range from team dinners to community service projects. Participating in these activities strengthens team bonds and creates lasting memories.

Reflecting and Learning

At the season's end, taking time to reflect on experiences, assess areas of improvement, and celebrate growth is crucial for setting future goals.

- Personal Reflection: Keep a journal throughout the season to record thoughts, feelings, achievements, and areas of difficulty. Reviewing this journal can provide insights into personal growth and highlight specific areas for future focus.
- Feedback Sessions: End-of-season meetings with coaches can offer valuable feedback. These discussions should cover strengths, areas for improvement, and suggestions for offseason activities to keep skills sharp.
- Goal Setting: Based on reflections and feedback, set goals for the next season. These might include specific skills to develop, mental aspects of the game to work on, or personal fitness goals. Setting these objectives provides motivation and a clear direction for improvement.
- Celebrate and Rest: After a season of hard work, it's important to take time to celebrate the achievements and rest. This downtime is essential for physical recovery and mental refreshment, preparing young players for future challenges and successes.

For young athletes embarking on their first baseball season, the experience is a mosaic of learning, growth, and fun. Through preparation, realistic expectations, building strong relationships, and reflective learning, players can navigate their inaugural season with confidence and enthusiasm. This approach not only enhances their skills and understanding of the game but also instills values and lessons that extend far beyond the baseball diamond.

CHAPTER 2
MASTERING THE BASICS

"What people don't realize is that professionals are sensational because of the fundamentals." – Barry Larkin

From the very first grip of the bat to the final victorious lap around the bases, the fundamentals of baseball act as the building blocks for every player's success. It's like learning the notes in a song or the steps in a dance; mastering the basics sets the stage for all the complex plays and strategies that make baseball the captivating sport it is. This chapter dives into the essential skills every young player needs to sharpen, from throwing with precision to catching with confidence, batting with power, and running bases with smart strategy. It's these core abilities that transform a group of players into a cohesive, formidable team.

2.1 THROWING TECHNIQUES FOR ACCURACY AND POWER

Throwing a baseball might seem straightforward at first glance, but there's an art to launching that ball with both strength and precision. Just like a well-aimed arrow needs both the right angle and the power behind it, a baseball throw combines technique with force, all starting with the grip and release, moving through body mechanics, and polished through practice drills.

Grip and Release

The way you grip the ball plays a crucial role in how it flies. Think of holding an egg; too tight, and it breaks, too loose, and you drop it. For a four-seam fastball, position your fingers across the seams, allowing for a straight, fast throw. This grip maximizes the ball's rotation, stabilizing its flight. The release, that moment the ball leaves your hand, should feel natural, like snapping a towel, using your fingers to add spin for accuracy.

- Exercise: Try gripping a baseball in different positions and notice how each grip feels in your hand. Practice tossing the ball lightly into the air, focusing on a comfortable, secure grip that allows for a smooth release.

Body Mechanics

Throwing power comes from more than just your arm; it's a full-body movement. Starting from your feet planted firmly on the ground, imagine your body as a coiled spring. As you begin the throw, uncoil by rotating your hips, then your shoulders, and finally your arm follows in a fluid motion. This sequence ensures the energy flows smoothly, amplifying the throw's power without straining your arm.

- Drill: Practice throwing with a focus on this sequence, starting slow to feel each part of your body engage. It's like learning a dance routine - first, get the steps right, then add speed and fluidity.

Drills for Improvement

Consistent practice is key to refining your throwing technique. A useful drill is the "knee drill" where you kneel on your throwing side knee, focusing purely on your upper body mechanics and arm strength. Another is the "long toss" where gradually increasing the distance of your throws builds both strength and accuracy.

- Checklist:
- Knee drill: 10 throws focusing on upper body movement.
- Long toss: Start at 10 feet, increasing by 5 feet after every 5 successful throws.

Common Mistakes and Corrections

Young players often make a few common mistakes, like "short-arming" the throw or releasing the ball too early or too late.

Short-arming, where the throw is made with a stiff elbow, reduces power and accuracy. Encouraging a full arm extension can correct this. For timing the release, practicing with a focus on how the ball feels at the moment of release helps in fine-tuning the timing for precise throws.

- Reflection Section: After a practice session, reflect on your throws. Did any feel particularly strong or accurate? Were there any you weren't happy with? What felt different about those throws?

By breaking down the throwing process, from the initial grip to the body's mechanics and the final release, players can start to understand how each element contributes to a successful throw. Like piecing together a puzzle, each part is essential, and when they all come together, the picture of a strong, accurate throw emerges. Through practice, reflection, and adjustments, young players can develop a throwing technique that serves as a reliable foundation for their game.

Moving beyond throwing, the next sections will explore other fundamental skills crucial for young players, including catching, batting, and base running. Each skill builds upon the other, creating a comprehensive skill set that enables players to confidently take on any position on the field.

2.2 CATCHING SKILLS: BUILDING CONFIDENCE AND SAFETY

Catching, a fundamental yet pivotal skill in baseball, requires not just quick reflexes but also a keen understanding of proper techniques. From the initial stance to the moment the ball hits the glove, each element plays a critical role in ensuring a successful catch. This section explores the intricacies of catching, highlighting the stance, glove position, and exercises designed to hone hand-eye coordination. Additionally, the correct use of safety equipment and a series of progressive drills aim to build both the skill and confidence necessary for young players to excel in this aspect of the game.

Proper Stance and Glove Position

A reliable catch starts with the correct stance. Feet should be shoulder-width apart, knees slightly bent, providing a stable and agile base. This position allows for quick movements in any direction, essential for reacting to the unpredictable path of a baseball. The glove, an extension of the hand, should be held in front, open and ready, signaling readiness to the pitcher and intimidating the batter. For balls in the air, raise the glove above your head, fingers pointed upward; for grounders, lower it to the ground, palm facing the incoming ball. These adjustments ensure that no matter where the ball is headed, you're prepared to meet it.

Hand-Eye Coordination Exercises

Enhancing hand-eye coordination is vital for developing catching skills. Simple exercises can make significant improvements. For instance:

- Barehand Toss: Without using a glove, gently toss a baseball from one hand to the other, gradually increasing the distance as your confidence grows. This drill sharpens focus and improves hand-eye coordination.

- Wall Ball: Throw a ball against a wall and catch it with your glove hand, focusing on watching the ball all the way into your glove. Vary the throw's speed and angle to practice different catch scenarios.

These exercises, when practiced consistently, refine the precision of your glove work, making every catch more assured.

Safety Equipment and Techniques

Catching comes with its risks, making safety equipment non-negotiable. A well-fitted glove provides not just a means to catch but also protection for the hand. Catchers, in particular, should wear additional gear: a helmet with a face mask, a chest protector, and leg guards. Each piece of equipment should fit snugly, offering maximum protection without hindering movement. Beyond wearing the right gear, adopting safe catching techniques is crucial. For instance, turning the head away from incoming high-speed throws to avoid facial injuries and learning to roll with the momentum of a catch to lessen the impact.

Progressive Catching Drills

Developing catching skills is a step-by-step process, best approached through progressive drills that build from simple to complex:

- Catch and Release: Start by having a partner throw the ball to you, focusing on securing the catch in your glove before quickly releasing it. Aim for smooth, fluid motions.
- Moving Target: As your confidence grows, incorporate movement. Run a short distance before catching a

thrown ball, mimicking game scenarios where you must move to make a catch.

- Pop Fly Practice: Use a machine or have a coach lob balls into the air, practicing your timing and glove positioning for catching high balls. This drill is excellent for overcoming the challenge of tracking and catching pop flies under pressure.

These drills, increasing in difficulty, ensure a gradual build-up of skill, preparing young players for the unpredictability and fast pace of live games.

Catching, with its blend of technical skill, physical readiness, and mental alertness, forms a cornerstone of defensive play in baseball. By dedicating time to mastering the stance, improving hand-eye coordination, adhering to safety protocols, and engaging in progressively challenging drills, young players can develop a reliable catching technique. This skill not only enhances their defensive capabilities but also builds the confidence necessary for success on the baseball field. Through consistent practice, attention to detail, and a focus on safety, the art of catching becomes an instinctive part of a player's repertoire, ready to be called upon in the heat of competition.

2.3 BATTING BASICS: TECHNIQUES FOR SUCCESSFUL HITS

The moment a bat connects with a ball, sending it soaring into the field, is one of baseball's most exhilarating experiences. Achieving this consistently, however, is where the challenge lies. It begins with a solid foundation in batting stance, grip, and swing mechanics—elements that, when combined correctly, turn potential energy into powerful hits.

Stance, Grip, and Swing Mechanics

A batter's stance is the groundwork for successful hitting. Feet should be shoulder-width apart, knees slightly bent, offering stability and readiness to move. The weight is balanced but ready to shift. Picture a coiled spring; that's the potential energy in a well-formed stance.

The grip on the bat is equally critical. Hands should come together smoothly around the bat, neither too tight nor too loose, allowing for quick, controlled movements. The V's formed by the thumbs and forefingers should align, ensuring a straight, powerful swing.

The swing itself is a blend of timing, power, and precision. It starts with the hips, not the arms, initiating a rotation that channels the body's power through the swing. The arms and bat follow, extending fully through the zone where the ball will pass. The goal is a fluid motion, from the coil of the stance through the uncoiling swing, ending in a balanced follow-through.

- A drill to refine this is the "tee work". Start with the ball on a batting tee adjusted to various heights and practice hitting with focus on form and follow-through.

Timing and Eye Coordination

Hitting a moving pitch requires impeccable timing and sharp eye coordination. The key here is anticipation and practice. Watching the pitcher's release point closely helps batters start their swing at the right moment. It's about syncing the body's motion with the ball's speed and trajectory.

- Practicing with a pitching machine set at different speeds can improve timing. Adjusting the machine to simulate different pitches trains the eye to follow the ball from release to bat contact.

Batting Drills for Practice

Drills are essential for translating batting theory into game-ready skills. Each practice session should have a clear focus, whether it's working on power, making contact, or refining swing mechanics.

- Soft Toss: A partner gently tosses balls to the batter from the side, focusing on making solid contact and following through.
- Front Toss: Similar to soft toss, but the balls are tossed from in front, allowing the batter to work on timing and tracking the ball into the contact zone.
- Bunting Drills: Though not about power, bunting requires precision and control, teaching batters to manage their bat and make deliberate contact.

Adjusting to Different Pitches

The ability to adapt to various pitches is what separates good hitters from great ones. Recognizing pitch types early gives batters the best chance to adjust their swing accordingly.

- For fastballs, the aim is to swing slightly earlier, meeting the ball squarely.

- Curveballs and sliders require patience, waiting longer for the ball to "break" before committing to the swing.

- Changeups, designed to deceive by mimicking a fastball's motion but at a slower speed, require batters to hold their swing a fraction longer.

Recognizing these pitches comes from experience and keen observation. Hitters can benefit from watching pitchers during games or on video, noting the differences in their delivery and arm action for each pitch type.

- Pitch Recognition Drills: Have a coach or machine simulate different pitches without the intention of hitting them. The focus is on identifying the pitch type and deciding in real-time whether it's a ball or a strike.

By breaking down batting into these fundamental components and dedicating time to practice and refine each aspect, players can develop a strong, reliable batting technique. This process is not about quick fixes but about building a foundation that allows for growth and adjustment as players face new challenges and higher levels of competition. Through diligent practice, a focus on the basics, and a commitment to continuous improvement, batters can step up to the plate with confidence, ready to make their mark on the game, one hit at a time.

2.4 BASE RUNNING: SPEED AND STRATEGY

In baseball, the path from base to base is more than just a sprint; it's a chess match played at full speed. The difference between a good base runner and a great one isn't just their quickness but their ability to make smart, strategic decisions in the heat of the moment. This section delves into the fundamentals of savvy base running, exploring the blend of speed, awareness, and tactics that can turn a simple hit into a scoring opportunity.

The Basics of Smart Base Running

Effective base running starts with a solid foundation in both physical speed and mental acuity. A smart base runner watches the game unfold, anticipating moves and looking for opportunities to advance. Key principles include:

- Lead-offs and Secondary Leads: Taking a calculated lead off the base can significantly shorten the distance to the next base, making a successful steal or advance on a hit more likely. A secondary lead, a small additional lead taken as the pitch is delivered, further optimizes this distance.

- Understanding Situational Baseball: Knowing the number of outs, the count on the batter, and the tendencies of the pitcher and fielders allows runners to make informed decisions about when to take risks and when to play it safe.

Stealing Bases

The art of stealing bases is a thrilling aspect of the game, requiring a blend of speed, timing, and the ability to read the pitcher. Successful steals often hinge on:

- Timing: Observing the pitcher's movements and finding a pattern or tell can give a base runner the edge they need to time their jump perfectly.

- Reading Pitchers: Different pitchers have different tells or motions that can indicate when they're about to throw to home plate versus when they're looking to pick off a runner. Recognizing these can be the difference between a stolen base and an out.
- Slide Techniques: A well-executed slide can evade tags and secure the base. Practicing different slide types—feet first, head first, or the pop-up slide—ensures runners are prepared for any situation.

Avoiding Tags and Making Safe Calls

Navigating around a tag requires agility and smarts. Runners can increase their chances of a safe call by:

- Running Paths: Choosing the most efficient path to the next base while being ready to adjust based on the fielder's position. Sometimes, a wider arc or a sudden change in direction can make all the difference.
- Effective Sliding: Beyond just evading tags, a good slide can help runners reach the base faster or avoid over-sliding. Practice and situational awareness determine the best type of slide to use in each scenario.

Base Running Drills

Improving base running skills involves a mix of speed training, agility drills, and situational practice. Some effective drills include:

- Suicide Sprints: Short, intense sprints that improve acceleration, an essential skill for stealing bases and taking extra bases on hits.

- Base-to-Base: Running from base to base with variations in speed and timing, simulating different game situations. Incorporating signals from a coach can mimic the need to react to in-game decisions.
- Sliding Practice: Using a sliding mat or a soft surface, practice various sliding techniques, focusing on form, speed, and how to protect oneself from injury.

Each of these components—smart decision-making, the daring dance of stealing bases, the craftiness in avoiding tags, and the rigorous preparation through drills—converges to form a well-rounded base runner. A player who not only possesses the speed to take advantage of opportunities but also the strategic mindset to create them. In the symphony of baseball, while the crack of the bat and the roar of the crowd might capture the most attention, the silent choreography of base running weaves its own narrative, punctuated by stolen moments and quiet triumphs that often spell the difference between victory and defeat.

2.5 POSITION-SPECIFIC TRAINING: UNDERSTANDING YOUR ROLE ON THE FIELD

In the dynamic world of baseball, every player has a unique role, each with its own set of responsibilities and skills. Grasping these roles is like unlocking different characters in a video game, where each one has special abilities and tasks to perform. This section will guide young players through understanding these roles, developing the specific skills needed for each position, and exploring drills that hone these abilities to perfection.

Roles and Responsibilities

On the baseball diamond, every position is a cog in a well-oiled machine, with each player contributing to the team's success in distinct ways.

- Pitchers are the strategists, controlling the game's tempo and battling batters with an arsenal of pitches.
- Catchers are the field generals, guiding pitchers, guarding home plate, and throwing out base runners attempting to steal.
- Infielders (First Baseman, Second Baseman, Shortstop, and Third Baseman) are the quick reactors, snagging ground balls and making swift throws to get runners out.
- Outfielders (Left Fielder, Center Fielder, Right Fielder) are the last line of defense, catching fly balls and stopping hits from turning into extra bases.

Each position demands a unique blend of physical and mental skills, from the pitcher's strategic thinking and precise control to the outfielder's speed and powerful arm.

Skills Development for Each Position

To excel in these roles, players must develop position-specific skills.

- Pitchers work on pitching mechanics, learning to throw various pitches with control and accuracy. Developing a repeatable delivery and understanding how to read batters are also key.
- Catchers focus on receiving pitches, blocking wild pitches, and throwing accuracy to nail base runners.

Strength training is crucial, as is practicing the quick transfer from glove to throwing hand.

- Infielders need agility and quick reflexes for fielding grounders and making rapid, accurate throws. They practice footwork for efficient fielding and turning double plays.
- Outfielders require speed to cover ground and arm strength for long, accurate throws back to the infield. They work on tracking fly balls and practicing relays for cutting down runners.

Position-Specific Drills

To sharpen these skills, tailored drills can make a significant difference.

- Pitchers might engage in bullpen sessions focusing on specific pitches, work on pickoff moves to control the running game, and simulate game situations to improve decision-making.
- Catchers could use drills to improve pop-up times, practice blocking techniques with balls in the dirt, and work on framing pitches to aid pitchers in getting strike calls.
- Infielders benefit from repetition drills for fielding ground balls at various angles, agility ladders for quick foot movement, and short hops to improve reaction times and soft hands.
- Outfielders might use long toss to build arm strength, drop step drills for better initial reactions to the ball off the bat, and tracking drills to read the ball's flight correctly.

These drills, when practiced consistently, not only improve the technical skills required for each position but also build the confidence needed to perform under pressure.

Transitioning Between Positions

Flexibility is a valuable trait in baseball, with players often moving between positions as they grow and as team needs change. Transitioning effectively requires understanding the new role's demands, from the strategic mindset of a pitcher to the reactive agility of an infielder.

Preparing for these transitions involves:

- Learning New Skills: Embracing the challenge of acquiring new abilities, whether it's a different way to field a ball or mastering the outfield's drop step.
- Mental Preparation: Understanding the responsibilities and decision-making processes specific to the new position. This might involve studying plays, positioning, and strategies.
- Physical Conditioning: Tailoring one's training to the demands of the new position. An infielder moving to the outfield, for example, might focus more on speed and endurance training.

Players often find that skills developed in one position can benefit another, making them more rounded athletes. The transition process, supported by coaches and teammates, can open new opportunities for personal growth and contribution to the team's success.

In the grand scheme of baseball, understanding and mastering one's role on the field is akin to a musician learning to play their part in an orchestra. Each position, with its unique responsibilities and required skills, contributes to the harmony of the team's performance. Through dedicated training, tailored drills, and the willingness to adapt and learn, young players can excel in their roles, bringing their best to the field every game. As they grow in their positions, they not only enhance their contributions to the team but also deepen their love and understanding of the game, ensuring a rewarding journey through the world of baseball.

2.6 DEVELOPING A STRONG DEFENSIVE GAME

In baseball, a strong defense can be as thrilling as a grand slam. It's the quiet guardian of the game's integrity, requiring players to blend anticipation, positioning, and seamless communication into a wall that challenges the opposing team's offense. This section unveils how young players can elevate their defensive game, turning routine plays into game-changing moments.

Fundamentals of Defense

At the heart of a formidable defense are three pillars: positioning, anticipation, and communication. Each player must know their role like the back of their hand, understanding not just where to be but also why. Positioning is about more than standing in a designated spot; it's about being in the right place at the right time, ready to spring into action. Anticipation is the skill of reading the game, predicting the ball's path before it leaves the bat. It's a chess game, where players think several moves ahead. Communication ties it all together. A silent field is a losing field. Players should be vocal, calling out plays, and alerting teammates to potential threats.

- Practice scenarios that focus on positioning, challenging players to position themselves correctly based on the number of outs and the runners on base.
- Simulate game situations that require players to anticipate the ball's movement, such as bunts or hit and runs.
- Encourage constant communication during practice games, rewarding players who effectively call out their actions and intentions.

Fielding Techniques

Proper fielding is the cornerstone of defense. For ground balls, players should approach with their body low to the ground, glove open and ready, creating a barrier that the ball can't sneak past. When facing fly balls, tracking the ball's trajectory is key, positioning the body so the ball can be caught at eye level, using two hands whenever possible for security. Line drives demand a quick reaction, with players needing to judge instantly whether to catch the ball on the fly or prepare for a bounce.

- Ground ball drills where players practice the "alligator catch" technique, scooping the ball into the glove and securing it with the bare hand.
- Fly ball drills under the sky or lights to improve tracking skills, focusing on catching with two hands.

- Line drive reaction drills, where players learn to judge the speed and path of the ball, deciding in an instant how to best field it.

Throwing for Defense

A strong arm is a valuable asset in baseball, but accuracy is what turns a throw into an out. Players must learn to throw with both power and precision, ensuring the ball reaches its target swiftly and securely. This starts with proper footwork, stepping towards the target to align the body for the throw. The arm motion should be fluid and controlled, releasing the ball at the right moment to send it on a direct path to the teammate's glove.

- Partner throwing drills that emphasize accuracy, challenging players to hit a target or their partner's chest consistently.
- Relay drills that simulate game throws from the outfield to the infield, focusing on quick, accurate throws to prevent base runners from advancing.

Defensive Drills and Scenarios

The best defense is one that acts as a single unit, with each player's actions seamlessly contributing to the team's strategy. Drills that mimic game scenarios can sharpen this collective instinct, preparing players for the pressures and challenges of real competition.

- "Situational defense" drills where players must react to specific game situations, such as runners on certain bases, different numbers of outs, or bunts.

- "Rapid fire" ground ball and fly ball drills that keep players moving and thinking on their feet, improving reaction times and decision-making under pressure.
- "Communication challenges" where players must complete defensive plays while also verbally coordinating with their teammates, enhancing the team's ability to work together smoothly.

In weaving these elements together, young players can elevate their defensive game, transforming it from a duty to a strategic advantage. With each practice, the anticipation becomes sharper, the positioning more intuitive, and the communication clearer. The field becomes a chessboard, and the defense, a set of players ready to make their move, turning the tide of the game with skill, strategy, and teamwork.

2.7 ADVANCED FIELDING STRATEGIES FOR THE YOUNG PLAYER

When young players step onto the baseball field, they're not just entering a physical space—they're stepping into a dynamic environment where every inch can make a difference in the game's outcome. To elevate their defensive game, players must go beyond basic skills, integrating advanced fielding strategies that leverage the field's dynamics, anticipate the ball's path, execute double plays with precision, and utilize teamwork to outmaneuver the opposition.

Understanding Field Dynamics

The baseball field is a stage, and each player is a performer with a specific role. Knowing the field's dynamics means understanding how the type of play, the batter's tendencies, and the game situation influence where a fielder positions themselves. For example, a shortstop might shift closer to second base when a fast runner is on first, ready for a double play ball. Similarly, outfielders adjust their depth based on the hitter's power and the likelihood of extra-base hits. Players who grasp these dynamics can position themselves optimally, ready to make plays that shift the game's momentum.

- Observing the batter's stance and swing can offer clues about the likely direction of the ball.
- Fielders should adjust their position based on the count; a hitter is more likely to swing for power on a favorable count, requiring fielders to adapt.

Anticipating the Ball's Path

Anticipation is key in transforming a good fielder into a great one. This skill involves reading the game's flow, the batter's behavior, and the pitch itself to predict where the ball might go. A curveball, for instance, might result in a grounder to the left side of the infield, while a fastball could lead to a fly ball. Players should also note the batter's timing—a late swing might send the ball to the opposite field. Training oneself to anticipate these outcomes allows for quicker reactions and more effective plays.

- Practice sessions should include varied pitching to batters to simulate different hitting scenarios.

- Fielders can improve their anticipation by paying close attention during batting practice, noting how different hits correlate with pitches and swings.

Double Plays and Advanced Techniques

Double plays are one of baseball's most thrilling defensive maneuvers, requiring precision, timing, and coordination. Mastering this technique not only boosts a team's defensive capability but also raises morale, snuffing out the opposing team's momentum. The key to a successful double play lies in quick, accurate throws and seamless communication between fielders. For infielders, this means perfecting the art of catching and releasing the ball swiftly while maintaining balance and control. Outfielders contribute by backing up bases and being ready to react if the ball is thrown away.

- Drill sequences that mimic game-like double play scenarios help build muscle memory and timing.
- Players should practice both as the initiator of the double play and as the receiver, ensuring smooth transitions regardless of their position in the play.

Utilizing Teamwork in Defense

Baseball, at its core, is a team sport, and nowhere is this more evident than in executing advanced defensive strategies. Effective communication and trust among teammates are crucial. Players must be vocal, calling out balls, directing plays, and alerting teammates to runners' positions. This collective awareness creates a defensive unit that's tough to beat. Team defense drills that emphasize group dynamics and communication can forge a cohesive unit, ready to back each other up and make split-second decisions that can change the game's outcome.

- Implementing team defense drills that simulate high-pressure situations helps build trust and improve communication.
- Encouraging players to talk through their thought process during these drills enhances mutual understanding and strategic coordination on the field.

In fielding, as in all aspects of baseball, the blend of individual skill and team synergy creates a defense that's both dynamic and robust. Players who understand the nuances of the field, anticipate the ball's path, execute complex plays like double plays with precision, and operate as a coordinated unit elevate the team's defensive prowess. This strategic depth adds layers to the game, making every play a testament to skill, preparation, and teamwork. As young players integrate these advanced strategies into their repertoire, they not only become more effective on the field but also deepen their appreciation for the game's complexities and the role each player plays in weaving the fabric of a successful team defense.

2.8 INCORPORATING EFFECTIVE PRACTICE DRILLS

Stepping onto the field, young players are not only embracing the game of baseball but also the opportunity to sculpt their skills, refine their strategies, and deepen their understanding of the game. The right practice routine, tailored to individual and team needs, becomes the blueprint for this growth. Here, we explore how to construct a practice routine that covers the game's many facets, drills that players can undertake solo to sharpen their abilities, team exercises that foster unity and strategic insight, and methods to track progress, ensuring every swing, pitch, and sprint adds to their development.

Designing a Practice Routine

A well-structured practice routine is akin to a map guiding players through the landscape of skill development. It should strike a balance between the various aspects of the game, ensuring equal attention to batting, fielding, base running, and mental strategy. The creation of this routine starts with a clear understanding of the team's goals and each player's individual objectives. From there:

- Allocate time segments for each skill area, adjusting based on immediate team needs or upcoming opponents.
- Incorporate warm-up and cool-down periods to prevent injuries and promote physical well-being.
- Plan for variability—different drills, changing focus areas—to keep practices engaging and challenging.
- Ensure there's room for both focused skill work and scrimmage play, the latter allowing players to apply skills in game-like scenarios.

Solo Drills for Skill Sharpening

While team practices are invaluable, individual drills allow players to hone specific skills at their own pace. These solo exercises can be tailored to address areas needing improvement or to strengthen already proficient skills.

- Batting Tee Work: Perfect for refining swing mechanics. Adjust the tee height and position to practice hitting pitches in various zones.
- Wall Throws: Ideal for improving throwing accuracy and arm strength. Mark targets on a wall at different heights and distances, practicing hitting these targets with throws.
- Glove Flips: Enhances fielding agility and hand-eye coordination. Toss a ball into the air and practice flipping it from the glove to the throwing hand as quickly and smoothly as possible.
- Shadow Running: Boosts base running skills. Without a ball in play, run through base paths, focusing on quick turns and slide techniques.

These drills, easily done in a backyard or park, empower players to take charge of their development, turning spare moments into opportunities for growth.

Team Drills for Cohesion

The chemistry of a baseball team can be the deciding factor in close games, making drills that enhance team cohesion and understanding essential. These exercises not only improve skills but also build the trust and communication vital for seamless play.

- Relay Races: Simulate game situations where quick, accurate throws are needed to get runners out. This drill emphasizes teamwork, communication, and precision.

- Bunt and Cover: Practices the coordination required during bunt plays. Pitchers, catchers, and infielders work together to field bunts and make plays, reinforcing strategic roles and responsibilities.
- Cut-off Drills: Focus on outfielders getting the ball into the infield quickly and infielders properly positioning themselves to relay the ball home, strengthening the team's defensive strategy.
- Pick-off Plays: Pitchers and infielders practice the timing and execution of pick-off moves, improving the team's ability to control the opposing team's base running.

By integrating these drills into practice sessions, teams can solidify their collective skills, ensuring that in the heat of competition, every player knows their role and trusts their teammates to fulfill theirs.

Measuring Progress

Tracking progress is crucial for maintaining motivation and ensuring that practice efforts translate into on-field performance. A few strategies for measuring development include:

- Skill Assessments: Regularly scheduled assessments can help track improvements in specific areas like batting average, fielding percentage, or pitching accuracy. Comparing these metrics over time offers a clear view of growth.
- Video Analysis: Recording practices and games gives players and coaches a visual tool to evaluate performance.

Reviewing footage can highlight areas of improvement and track changes in technique.

- Personal Journals: Encouraging players to keep practice journals allows for self-reflection. Entries can note what felt good during practice, areas of struggle, and personal feelings about progress, providing a holistic view of a player's journey.

- Feedback Sessions: Regular meetings between coaches and players to discuss progress, set new goals, and adjust practice routines ensure that efforts are aligned with desired outcomes.

Incorporating these measurement methods into the practice routine provides tangible evidence of improvement, reinforcing the value of hard work and dedication. It turns practice from a routine into a journey of continuous growth, with each session building towards the ultimate goal of becoming not just better players but students of the game, always eager to learn, adjust, and improve.

2.9 UTILIZING VIDEO ANALYSIS FOR SKILL IMPROVEMENT

In today's digitally-driven world, the use of video analysis has become a game-changer in sports, offering a lens through which players can view their actions with an analytical eye. This tool allows for a detailed examination of techniques, providing insights that are not always perceivable in the heat of the moment. For young baseball players striving to refine their skills, video analysis stands as an invaluable resource.

Benefits of Video Analysis

The advantages of incorporating video analysis into training routines are manifold. Primarily, it offers an objective perspective of a player's performance, highlighting both strengths and areas needing enhancement. Video replay can capture nuances missed during live action—be it a slight hitch in a batting swing or a minor misstep in fielding positioning. Moreover, this method fosters self-awareness among young athletes, encouraging them to take ownership of their development through visual feedback.

- Allows for a detailed review of techniques and mechanics
- Encourages self-assessment and fosters a proactive approach to skill improvement
- Enhances the understanding of game dynamics and personal performance within that context

How to Record and Analyze

Capturing useful footage doesn't require sophisticated equipment; a smartphone or a basic digital camera can suffice. The key lies in the positioning—ensuring a clear, unobstructed view of the action. For batting analysis, a side angle can best reveal the mechanics of the swing. In contrast, a behind-the-catcher perspective offers insight into a pitcher's delivery and movement. When reviewing the footage, focus on specific aspects of performance rather than watching passively. Look for consistency in mechanics, reaction times, and decision-making processes.

- Use a tripod or have a steady hand to avoid shaky footage
- Record from various angles to capture different aspects of gameplay

- Review the footage soon after recording to connect the visual feedback with the muscle memory of the actions

Identifying Areas for Improvement

The critical evaluation of video footage can unearth subtle yet impactful adjustments that can elevate a player's game. For pitchers, it might reveal inconsistencies in the release point or stride length. Batters may notice timing issues or unnecessary movements that hinder their swing. The objective is not to overhaul a player's style but to fine-tune and enhance efficiency. Creating a highlight reel of both successful and less effective plays can serve as a visual guide for what to replicate and what to adjust.

- Focus on one aspect at a time to avoid information overload
- Compare footage over time to track progress and regression
- Engage with a coach or a mentor in the review process for expert insights

Incorporating Feedback into Practice

The insights gleaned from video analysis should directly inform practice routines. If a batter identifies a tendency to drop the shoulder during a swing, targeted drills can be incorporated into training sessions to address this issue. For pitchers struggling with accuracy, focusing on consistent release points during bullpen sessions can be beneficial. The key is to translate the visual feedback into actionable practice goals, creating a loop of performance, analysis, and improvement.

- Set specific, measurable objectives based on video analysis findings
- Integrate corrective exercises and drills into regular practice sessions
- Regularly record and review performance to monitor progress and adjust training focus as needed

In weaving video analysis into the fabric of training and development, young baseball players unlock a powerful tool for self-improvement. This method not only sharpens skills but also deepens their understanding of the game's intricacies. It cultivates a reflective, analytical mindset, encouraging players to continuously seek ways to elevate their performance. As they progress, the benefits of this approach extend beyond individual achievement, contributing to the collective strength and success of their teams.

By embracing video analysis, players embark on a path of relentless improvement, where each review session holds the promise of discovery and advancement. This journey, guided by the clear, objective lens of the camera, paves the way for young athletes to reach their full potential, transforming potential into prowess one frame at a time.

As we close this chapter on mastering the basics, it's clear that the journey to excellence in baseball is one of ongoing learning and refinement. The tools and strategies discussed here—from the meticulousness of video analysis to the rigor of targeted drills—serve as the foundation upon which players can build a robust set of skills. Moving forward, the focus shifts from the individual to the collective, exploring how teamwork and strategy play pivotal roles in achieving success on the baseball field.

CHAPTER 3
BUILDING MENTAL FORTITUDE IN BASEBALL

"The more you play baseball, the less depends on your athletic ability. It's a mental war more than anything." – Alex Rodriguez

Imagine standing at the plate, bat in hand, with the game on the line. Your heart races, your palms sweat, and the roar of the crowd fades until it's just you and the pitcher, locked in a silent duel. In this moment, it's not just your physical skills that will determine the outcome, but your mental toughness. Similarly, envision being on the mound, the bases loaded, and it's up to you to protect a slender lead. Here, your mindset can be your greatest ally or your toughest opponent. This chapter is about nurturing that ally, transforming pressure into fuel, setbacks into lessons, and challenges into opportunities.

In baseball, mental toughness isn't a bonus; it's a necessity. It's what separates those who dream big from those who achieve greatness. Let's explore how young athletes can build this critical skill set, transforming their mental approach to excel both on and off the diamond.

Understanding Mental Toughness

Mental toughness in youth baseball is the inner strength that helps players face and overcome the pressures, challenges, and adversities of the game. It's about staying focused on the pitch, not the scoreboard. This resilience, focus, and unwavering belief in one's abilities are what enable players to perform at their best, especially under pressure.

- Resilience allows players to bounce back from errors, bad calls, or tough losses.
- Focus keeps their minds on the present, not dwelling on past mistakes or worrying about future outcomes.
- Self-confidence is believing in their skills and preparation, even when faced with formidable opponents.

Building Blocks of Mental Toughness

Developing mental toughness involves more than just wishful thinking; it requires deliberate practice and cultivation of specific traits. Here are the core components:

- Self-Confidence: Confidence isn't something you're born with; it's built through hard work, success, and even failure. Celebrating small victories, mastering new skills, and positive self-talk can bolster a player's belief in their abilities.

- Focus: In a game as nuanced as baseball, maintaining focus amidst distractions (cheering fans, jeering opponents) is crucial. Techniques like setting mini-goals for each game or at-bat can help players stay engaged and present.
- Determination: The drive to improve, to push through tough practices, and to strive for better performance is what determination is all about. It's about setting challenging yet achievable goals and relentlessly pursuing them.

Strategies for Developing Mental Toughness

Building mental toughness is like building muscle; it takes time, effort, and consistency. Here are practical ways players can strengthen their mental game:

- Goal Setting: Start with clear, specific goals for both practice and games. Break them down into achievable steps. This gives players a roadmap to follow, with each small success building confidence and motivation.
- Positive Self-Talk: Encourage players to become aware of their inner dialogue. Transform negative thoughts into positive affirmations. Instead of thinking, "I can't hit this pitcher," try, "I'm ready and capable of getting a hit."
- Visualization: Spend time visualizing successful outcomes, whether it's making contact with the ball, executing the perfect pitch, or making a game-saving catch. This mental rehearsal can enhance performance and reduce game-day nerves.

Overcoming Mental Barriers

Even with strong mental toughness, players will encounter mental barriers. Recognizing and overcoming these are part of the growth process:

- Fear of Failure: This is a common barrier that can paralyze players, making them too afraid to take risks. Remind them that baseball is a game of failure; even the best hitters fail seven out of ten times. It's not about avoiding failure but learning from it.

- Losing Focus: Distractions, both on and off the field, can derail a player's game. Techniques like deep breathing, focusing on one pitch at a time, and having a pre-at-bat routine can help maintain focus.

- Pressure: The weight of expectations can be overwhelming. Simplifying the game to its basics, focusing on effort over outcome, and practicing mindfulness can help players manage pressure.

Building mental toughness is a journey, not a destination. It requires patience, practice, and persistence. But the rewards—increased confidence, improved performance, and a greater love for the game—make the journey well worth it.

In baseball, every player will face moments of adversity, whether it's a slump at the plate, a challenging opponent, or a high-pressure situation. These moments test not just their skills but their mental fortitude. The strategies outlined here provide a starting point for players to develop the mental toughness needed to navigate these challenges successfully. By setting realistic goals, practicing positive self-talk, visualizing success, and learning from setbacks, young athletes can build the mental resilience necessary to thrive in baseball and beyond.

3.2 STRATEGIES FOR OVERCOMING PERFORMANCE ANXIETY

The crack of the bat, the cheer of the crowd, and the rush of the game can sometimes transform into a high-pressure cooker for young athletes, where performance anxiety lurks behind each play. In this part of our exploration, we dive into understanding and managing performance anxiety, ensuring it doesn't stand in the way of enjoying and excelling in baseball.

Identifying Signs of Performance Anxiety

First, it's vital to spot the telltale signs of performance anxiety in young athletes. These symptoms can range from physical to psychological:

- Physical Symptoms: Noticeable changes such as shaky hands, rapid heartbeat, excessive sweating, or even nausea before or during games.
- Psychological Symptoms: Increased feelings of doubt, fear of letting the team down, or an overwhelming sense of pressure can signal anxiety. Also, watch for changes in behavior, like withdrawal from teammates or a reluctance to participate in plays they usually enjoy.

Root Causes of Anxiety in Sports

Understanding the root causes of performance anxiety can illuminate strategies to manage it. Common sources include:

- Fear of Failure: At its core, much of the anxiety stems from a fear of not meeting expectations—be it their own, their teammates', or those of parents and coaches.
- Lack of Preparation: Feeling underprepared can also trigger anxiety. This isn't always about the quantity of practice but the quality and focus of that preparation.
- Previous Negative Experiences: Past mistakes or losses, especially those that had significant emotional impact, can haunt players, making them anxious about repeating those errors.

Identifying these triggers is the first step toward managing them effectively.

Techniques to Manage Anxiety Before and During Games

Several strategies can help young players manage their anxiety, allowing them to focus on the joy and challenge of the game:

- Breathing Exercises: Simple yet effective, deep breathing can help calm the nerves. Encourage players to take deep, slow breaths before the game and during tense moments, focusing on the rise and fall of their chest.
- Progressive Muscle Relaxation (PMR): Tension often accompanies anxiety. PMR involves tensing and then relaxing different muscle groups, promoting physical and mental relaxation.
- Visualization: Similar to mental rehearsals for skill improvement, visualization can be used to imagine positive outcomes, such as executing a perfect swing or

making a crucial catch, helping to build confidence and reduce anxiety.

- Routine Development: Creating a pre-game routine can provide a sense of control and normalcy, reducing anxiety. This routine can include physical warm-ups, mental preparation techniques, or even a specific sequence of actions leading up to the game.

Creating a Supportive Environment

The role of coaches and parents in creating a supportive environment that reduces performance anxiety cannot be overstated:

- Emphasize Effort Over Outcome: Shifting the focus from winning to effort and improvement can alleviate the pressure to perform perfectly. Celebrate the hard work and progress, not just the scoreboard.
- Open Communication: Foster an environment where players feel comfortable expressing their fears and anxieties. Listen actively and provide reassurance that it's normal to feel nervous.
- Educate About Anxiety: Sharing information about performance anxiety and its commonality can normalize the experience, making players less likely to feel isolated or overwhelmed by their feelings.
- Encourage a Team Support System: Cultivate a team culture where players support each other, recognizing that they all face similar pressures and can rely on each other for encouragement and understanding.

Incorporating these strategies into the fabric of youth baseball can help players manage performance anxiety effectively. By recognizing the signs, understanding the causes, employing techniques to manage anxiety, and creating a supportive environment, young athletes can step onto the field with confidence, ready to face whatever the game throws at them with determination and a clear mind.

3.3 THE POWER OF POSITIVE THINKING AND VISUALIZATION

Stepping up to the plate or taking the mound in a crucial moment of the game requires more than just physical preparedness; it demands a powerful ally—your mind. The realms of positive thinking and visualization are not just abstract concepts but practical tools that, when wielded with intent, can significantly elevate a young baseball player's game.

Benefits of Positive Thinking

The impact of positive thinking on performance is profound. It's the fuel that powers perseverance, ignites motivation, and builds resilience. Here's how it shapes a player:

- Boosts Confidence: Believing in one's abilities shifts focus from doubts to strengths, paving the way for confident, assertive play.
- Enhances Motivation: Positive thinking turns challenges into stepping stones, driving players to push beyond their limits.

- Strengthens Resilience: It equips players to bounce back from setbacks, viewing them as opportunities for growth rather than insurmountable obstacles.

Cultivating a Positive Mindset

Fostering a positive mindset in young athletes is akin to planting a seed that, with care, grows into a steadfast source of strength and optimism. Here are strategies to nurture this mindset:

- Acknowledge Progress: Recognize and celebrate even the smallest improvements. This acknowledgment reinforces the belief that effort leads to growth.
- Encourage Self-Reflection: After games or practices, encourage players to list three things they did well. This practice shifts focus to positives, gradually building a habit of looking for the silver lining.
- Frame Challenges Positively: Teach players to see challenges as chances to learn. Replacing "I can't" with "I haven't yet" transforms obstacles into potential victories.
- Create a Team Culture of Positivity: Cultivate an environment where encouragement, support, and positive reinforcement are the norms. This collective positivity can have a transformative effect on individual mindsets.

Introduction to Visualization Techniques

Visualization, or mental rehearsal, is the practice of creating vivid, positive mental images of success before it happens. It's a technique used by athletes worldwide to mentally prepare for competition, enhancing performance by imagining successful outcomes.

- Clarifies Goals: Visualization helps players clearly see their objectives, making goals more tangible and achievable.
- Prepares for Success: By mentally rehearsing successful plays, players prime their bodies and minds for actual performance, reducing anxiety and improving focus.
- Builds Confidence: Regular visualization of success builds a deep-seated belief in one's ability to perform under pressure.

Practical Exercises for Visualization

Implementing visualization into a young athlete's routine can be straightforward and immensely beneficial. Here are exercises to start:

1. Pre-Game Visualization:
   - Find a quiet space before games or practice.
   - Close your eyes and take deep breaths to relax.
   - Imagine walking onto the field, feeling the bat in your hands, or positioning yourself on the mound.
   - Visualize the pitch coming towards you, swinging the bat with perfect timing, and making solid contact, watching as the ball flies exactly where you intended.
   - Feel the success, the cheers, and the satisfaction of a play well-executed.
   - Open your eyes, carrying that confidence with you onto the field.

2. Post-Practice Reflection:
   - After practice, take a moment to reflect on what you've worked on.
   - Close your eyes and replay the best moments, focusing on what you did right. Feel the movement, the decisions, and the outcomes.
   - Embed these positive experiences in your memory, ready to be drawn upon during games.

3. Visualization of Goals:
   - Set aside time weekly to visualize your long-term goals.
   - Imagine achieving your season's objectives, whether it's improving your batting average, mastering a new pitch, or helping your team win a championship.
   - Feel the joy, pride, and satisfaction of achieving these goals, using this positive energy to fuel your motivation and effort.

4. Overcoming Challenges:
   - Think of a recent challenge or setback.
   - Visualize yourself facing this challenge again, but this time, overcome it successfully. Whether it's hitting a challenging pitch or making a difficult catch, see yourself succeeding effortlessly.
   - Use this visualization to transform doubts into confidence, ready to tackle any challenge on the field.

Incorporating these visualization exercises into a young player's routine can have a significant impact on their mental approach to the game. By fostering a positive mindset and regularly engaging in mental rehearsals of success, players can step onto the field well-prepared, not just physically but mentally and emotionally. This preparation doesn't guarantee success in every at-bat or game, but it equips players with the mental tools to face whatever comes their way with confidence, resilience, and a positive outlook, setting the foundation for both personal and team triumphs.

3.4 COPING WITH LOSS AND SETBACKS: A GUIDE FOR YOUNG PLAYERS

In the vibrant landscape of youth baseball, every player, at some point, faces the sting of a loss or the frustration of a setback. These moments, though tough, are woven into the fabric of the sport, providing fertile ground for growth, resilience, and a deeper understanding of the game's true essence. This section aims to shine a light on navigating these challenges, transforming them from sources of disappointment into catalysts for development.

Normalizing Failure and Loss

The first step in building resilience is to reframe how we view failure and loss. In baseball, as in life, setbacks are not detours but part of the journey towards excellence. It's crucial to communicate that even the most celebrated baseball legends experienced failures and setbacks. They are not markers of inadequacy but milestones in learning and progress.

- Shared Experiences: Highlight stories of professional players who turned their failures into stepping stones for success. This not only humanizes these icons but also shows young athletes that setbacks are universal and surmountable.

- Embrace a Growth Mindset: Instill the belief that abilities and talents can be developed through dedication and hard work. A loss is simply feedback, an opportunity to learn and improve.

Learning from Loss

The true value of a setback lies in the lessons it imparts. Each game, each at-bat, and each pitch offers insights that, when harnessed, can significantly enhance a player's future performance. Encouraging young athletes to adopt a reflective approach post-game allows them to identify both strengths to build upon and areas needing improvement.

- Reflection Sessions: After games, particularly those that didn't go as hoped, hold sessions where players can reflect on their performance in a supportive environment. Discuss what went well and what could be done differently next time.
- Constructive Feedback: Provide specific, actionable feedback that focuses on performance improvement. This helps players see their potential for growth rather than dwelling on the loss.

Building Resilience After Failure

Resilience is the ability to bounce back from setbacks with renewed vigor and confidence. Developing this quality in young athletes equips them with the emotional robustness to face future challenges head-on.

- Set Short-Term Goals: After a setback, help players set achievable goals for the next game or practice. This redirects focus towards positive action and away from rumination.

- Encourage Routine: Maintaining a consistent practice routine fosters a sense of normalcy and control, which can be comforting after a loss. It's a reminder that progress is a continuous process, independent of a single game's outcome.

- Support Network: Cultivate a team atmosphere where players support each other, celebrating successes and offering encouragement during tough times. Knowing they're not alone in their journey can significantly bolster a player's resilience.

Role of Coaches and Parents in the Recovery Process

The influence of coaches and parents in guiding young athletes through the aftermath of a loss is monumental. Their support can shape how players perceive failure and their ability to recover from it.

- Offer Perspective: Remind players that baseball is a game of failures, where even the best have their off days. What matters is the passion and effort they bring to the field every day.

- Active Listening: Sometimes, all a player needs is someone to listen without judgment. Be there to hear their frustrations and disappointments, validating their feelings without immediately jumping to solutions.

- Encouragement: Reinforce the message that their worth isn't tied to wins or losses but in their dedication, teamwork, and the joy they bring to the game.
- Model Resilience: Demonstrate through your actions and words what it means to face setbacks with grace and determination. How adults handle failure can profoundly influence how young players cope with their own challenges.

In navigating losses and setbacks, the essential lesson for young players is that these experiences, though painful, are not the end but the beginning. They are opportunities cloaked in disguise, offering invaluable lessons, fostering resilience, and deepening a player's love and understanding of the game. Through thoughtful reflection, goal setting, and the unwavering support of coaches and parents, young athletes can learn to view each setback not as a roadblock but as a stepping stone towards their goals. This shift in perspective is what transforms a good player into a great one, imbuing them with the strength, wisdom, and character to face any challenge baseball or life throws their way.

3.5 EMOTIONAL INTELLIGENCE: MANAGING EMOTIONS FOR BETTER PLAY

In the vibrant world of youth baseball, where the crack of the bat and the cheer of the crowds fill the air, lies an often-overlooked aspect of the game: emotional intelligence. This section shines a light on the profound impact emotional intelligence has on young athletes, transforming how they interact with teammates, approach the game, and ultimately, how they play.

The Role of Emotional Intelligence in Sports

Emotional intelligence, the ability to understand and manage your emotions and those of others, plays a pivotal role in the dynamics of youth baseball. It's this understanding and management that can mean the difference between a team that crumbles under pressure and one that thrives. In the context of youth baseball, it's about recognizing the frustration of a missed catch or the anxiety of batting with bases loaded and using that awareness to make constructive decisions.

- It's the player who takes a deep breath and refocuses after a strikeout, rather than spiraling into a cycle of self-criticism.
- It's the teammate who notices a fellow player's disappointment and offers a word of encouragement, strengthening team cohesion.
- It's the coach who reads the mood of the team and tailors their pep talk to either uplift spirits or calm nerves.

Recognizing and Regulating Emotions

For young athletes, learning to recognize and regulate emotions lays the groundwork for emotional intelligence. It starts with fostering an environment where emotions are acknowledged and expressed healthily.

- Emotion Recognition: Teach players to identify what they're feeling. Is it nerves, frustration, excitement? Naming the emotion is the first step in managing it.

- Emotion Regulation: Once identified, strategies such as focused breathing, positive self-talk, or even a brief moment of mindfulness can help manage these emotions, keeping players' heads in the game.

Empathy and Team Dynamics

Empathy, the ability to understand and share the feelings of another, is the glue that holds teams together. It encourages a supportive environment where players feel valued and understood, which is crucial for young athletes.

- When a player shows empathy, it can transform team dynamics, making way for a more cohesive unit. A simple gesture of understanding, whether it's a pat on the back after a mistake or a shared celebration of a win, can significantly impact morale.

- This empathy fosters open communication, where players feel comfortable sharing their thoughts and feelings, knowing they will be met with understanding, not judgment.

Exercises to Improve Emotional Intelligence

Developing emotional intelligence is a process, one that requires intention and practice. Here are some exercises designed to enhance this critical skill set in young baseball players:

- Reflective Listening: Pair players up and have them share a recent experience from a game or practice. The listener's goal is to reflect back what they've heard, focusing on understanding the speaker's perspective and emotions. This exercise fosters empathy and active listening skills.

- Emotion Labeling: During team meetings, encourage players to share how they felt during specific moments in recent games. Was there a moment of pride, disappointment, joy, or frustration? Labeling these emotions in a supportive setting helps players become more attuned to their emotional states and those of their teammates.

- Group Problem-Solving: Present the team with a hypothetical challenging scenario, perhaps a game where things aren't going well. As a group, discuss how to handle the situation emotionally and strategically. This promotes empathy by considering different perspectives and emotional intelligence by navigating the feelings involved in problem-solving.

- Mindfulness Moments: Start or end practices with a brief mindfulness exercise, focusing on the breath or a moment of gratitude. This practice can help players center themselves, manage stress, and cultivate a positive state of mind.

In weaving emotional intelligence into the fabric of youth baseball, players gain more than just improved performance on the field; they acquire skills that will serve them well beyond the diamond. Learning to manage emotions, to empathize with teammates, and to navigate the highs and lows with grace not only creates better athletes but better individuals. Through dedicated practice, reflection, and the support of coaches and parents, young players can develop the emotional intelligence necessary to face whatever the game, or life, throws their way.

3.6 NUTRITION AND HYDRATION TIPS FOR YOUNG BASEBALL PLAYERS

Nurturing the body with the right fuel and keeping it well-hydrated are as crucial to a young baseball player's performance as mastering the perfect swing or pitch. This section aims to offer valuable insights into how young athletes can optimize their nutrition and hydration to support their growth, training, and game-day performance.

Importance of Proper Nutrition

A well-balanced diet is foundational for young athletes, providing the energy needed for high-level performance and supporting physical growth and development. Nutrients like carbohydrates fuel muscles during intense activities, while proteins are essential for muscle repair and recovery. Fats, often misunderstood, play a vital role in long-term energy storage and cell structure. Together, these macronutrients, along with essential vitamins and minerals, ensure that young players have the stamina, strength, and focus needed both on and off the field.

Basic Nutritional Guidelines

Navigating the world of nutrition can be daunting, but a few basic guidelines can simplify this process:

- Macronutrient Balance: Aim for a diet consisting of about 55-60% carbohydrates, 15-20% protein, and 25-30% fats. This balance ensures a steady energy supply and supports muscle growth and recovery.
- Fruits and Vegetables: These are rich sources of vitamins, minerals, and antioxidants, crucial for immune function and overall health. Encourage colorful plates at every meal for a wide range of nutrients.
- Whole Grains: Opt for whole grains over refined grains to provide sustained energy and essential fibers, which aid in digestion and keep you feeling fuller longer.
- Lean Proteins: Incorporate a variety of lean proteins, including poultry, fish, beans, and legumes, to support muscle repair and growth.
- Healthy Fats: Sources like avocados, nuts, seeds, and olive oil contribute to brain health and energy levels without weighing you down.

Hydration Strategies

Hydration is another key component of athletic performance, often overlooked until thirst kicks in, by which time dehydration may have already started to set in. Dehydration can significantly impair performance, reducing strength, stamina, and cognitive function. Here are strategies to ensure young players stay adequately hydrated:

- Before Activity: Encourage drinking 16-20 ounces of water at least two hours before exercise, allowing time for absorption and for any excess to be excreted.
- During Activity: Sip 7-10 ounces of water every 10-20 minutes during activity. In hot weather or during longer games and practices, a sports drink with electrolytes can help replace lost salts in addition to providing hydration.
- After Activity: Rehydrate with 16-24 ounces of water for every pound lost during activity. Monitoring urine color can be a practical way to gauge hydration levels, aiming for a light straw color.

Sample Meal and Snack Ideas

To make nutrition and hydration more approachable for young athletes, here are some practical meal and snack ideas that are both nutritious and easy to prepare:

- Breakfast: Oatmeal topped with fresh fruit and a dollop of peanut butter for a mix of complex carbs, protein, and healthy fats.
- Lunch: A turkey and avocado wrap with whole grain tortillas, offering a perfect blend of lean protein, healthy fats, and fiber.
- Dinner: Grilled chicken or tofu, quinoa, and a side of steamed vegetables drizzled with olive oil, providing a balanced meal to support recovery and growth.
- Snacks: Yogurt with mixed berries and a handful of almonds; hummus with sliced carrots and celery; or a

banana with a small handful of trail mix are excellent options for quick, energy-boosting snacks.

- Hydration: Aside from water, coconut water can be a natural alternative for rehydration, offering electrolytes like potassium and magnesium with less sugar than most sports drinks.

Incorporating these nutrition and hydration strategies into a young baseball player's routine can profoundly impact their energy levels, performance, and overall health. By fueling their bodies with the right nutrients and maintaining proper hydration, young athletes set the stage not only for success in baseball but for a lifetime of healthy habits.

3.7 INJURY PREVENTION AND MANAGEMENT: STAYING IN THE GAME

Playing baseball, much like any sport, comes with its fair share of risks. For young athletes, who are still growing and developing, understanding how to prevent injuries is key to enjoying the game to its fullest. This section explores common injuries in youth baseball, how to prevent them, and the steps to take if an injury occurs, ensuring players stay safe and healthy on their path to becoming seasoned athletes.

Common Baseball Injuries and Their Causes

In the realm of youth baseball, certain injuries surface more frequently due to the repetitive and sometimes strenuous nature of the sport. Recognizing these common injuries is the first step in prevention and management.

- Throwing Injuries: Often affecting the shoulder and elbow, these injuries stem from the overuse of muscles, tendons, and ligaments. The repetitive motion of throwing, especially without proper technique or rest, can lead to conditions such as Little League elbow or shoulder.
- Fielding Injuries: Sprains, strains, and bruises are common among players who field, mainly due to sudden movements, collisions, or improper handling of the ball.
- Baserunning Injuries: Sliding into bases and sudden sprints can result in ankle sprains, hamstring strains, and even fractures if not executed correctly.

Understanding these injuries' causes underscores the importance of proper technique, physical conditioning, and mindful play.

Preventive Measures

Preventing injuries is far more effective than treating them. Here are several strategies and exercises aimed at keeping young players healthy:

- Proper Warm-Up Routines: Begin each practice and game with a dynamic warm-up. Activities should include light jogging, leg swings, arm circles, and gentle stretching to prepare the body for the demands of baseball.
- Strength Training for Injury-Prone Areas: Focus on exercises that strengthen the muscles around the shoulder, elbow, and knees. Bodyweight exercises, resistance bands,

or light weights can be used, emphasizing proper form over heavy lifting.

- Pitch Count Limits: Adhering to pitch count guidelines helps protect young arms from overuse. Ensuring players have adequate rest between pitching appearances is also crucial.

- Teaching Proper Techniques: From throwing to batting and sliding, correct techniques not only improve performance but also reduce the risk of injury. Coaches should regularly instruct and correct players on the fundamentals of each movement.

- Encouraging Cross-Training: Engaging in different sports outside of baseball season can enhance overall fitness, flexibility, and reduce the risk of overuse injuries.

First Aid and When to Seek Medical Attention

Even with preventive measures in place, injuries can still occur. Knowing how to respond can make a significant difference in the recovery process.

- Immediate Care for Minor Injuries (R.I.C.E.): For sprains, strains, and bruises, the R.I.C.E. method (Rest, Ice, Compression, Elevation) is effective for initial treatment. This approach helps reduce swelling and pain in the injured area.

- Recognizing Serious Injuries: Symptoms such as severe pain, swelling that doesn't reduce with R.I.C.E., inability to move or put weight on the injured area, or visible deformities are signs that medical attention is needed.

- Concussion Awareness: Any head injury should be taken seriously. Symptoms like confusion, headache, dizziness, or loss of consciousness warrant immediate medical evaluation.

Returning to Play After Injury

The journey back to the field after an injury should be gradual and carefully managed to prevent re-injury.

- Follow Medical Advice: Always adhere to the recommendations provided by healthcare professionals regarding rest and rehabilitation.
- Gradual Return to Activity: Begin with light activities that do not stress the injured area. Gradually increase the intensity and volume of play as strength and flexibility return.
- Physical Rehabilitation: Engage in specific exercises and treatments prescribed by a physical therapist to restore function, improve strength, and ensure the injury heals correctly.
- Mental Readiness: An often-overlooked aspect of returning to play is the athlete's mental state. Fear of re-injury can hinder performance. Mental readiness involves rebuilding confidence in the body's ability to perform and trust in the recovery process. Players might benefit from visualization techniques, focusing on successful play without discomfort or hesitation.

Injury prevention and management are as integral to the game as hitting and pitching. By educating young players on common injuries and their causes, implementing preventive measures, providing prompt and appropriate care for injuries, and managing the return-to-play process thoughtfully, we ensure that the path to baseball excellence is both safe and rewarding. Through these practices, young athletes can enjoy the game they love while minimizing the risks, staying healthy, and developing into well-rounded, resilient players.

3.8 THE IMPORTANCE OF REST AND RECOVERY

In the high-energy, always-on world of youth baseball, taking time to rest and recover might seem like a pause in progress. However, it's during these quieter moments that young athletes' bodies and minds rejuvenate, paving the way for peak performance when it matters most. This section lays out the why and how of incorporating rest and recovery into a young player's routine, ensuring they remain at the top of their game throughout the season.

Rest is not merely a break from training; it's an active component of an athlete's development process. It allows for physical repair, mental clarity, and performance enhancement. Muscles stressed during practice rebuild stronger during rest periods, mental fatigue eases, and the consolidation of skills occurs, leading to improved execution during the game.

Recognizing Signs of Overtraining

It's crucial for players, coaches, and parents to be vigilant for signs of overtraining, which can derail even the most dedicated athlete. These signs include:

- Persistent fatigue that doesn't improve with regular rest
- Decreased performance despite increased training intensity
- Mood swings or increased irritability
- Difficulty sleeping or changes in appetite
- Increased incidence of injuries or illnesses

Identifying these early allows for timely intervention, preventing more severe impacts on health and performance.

Strategies for Effective Recovery

Effective recovery strategies are as varied as the athletes themselves, encompassing physical, mental, and emotional aspects. Here are a few key approaches:

- Sleep Hygiene: Quality sleep is the cornerstone of recovery. Encouraging consistent sleep schedules, creating a restful environment, and limiting screen time before bed can significantly improve sleep quality.
- Active Recovery Days: Intersperse training days with active recovery, which involves light, non-strenuous activities like walking, yoga, or gentle stretching. This keeps the body moving and aids in muscle recovery without the intensity of regular training.
- Stress Management Techniques: Baseball, school, and social commitments can all contribute to stress. Techniques such as mindfulness, deep breathing exercises, or engaging in hobbies can help manage stress levels, contributing to overall well-being and readiness to play.

- Nutritional Recovery: Adequate hydration and a balanced diet rich in nutrients support the body's repair mechanisms. Incorporating protein for muscle repair, carbohydrates for energy replenishment, and antioxidants to combat inflammation can aid in physical recovery.

Balancing Training and Rest

Finding the right balance between training intensity, volume, and rest is key to sustainable athletic development. Here are some considerations for achieving this balance:

- Listen to the Body: Encourage young athletes to tune into their bodies, recognizing when they feel energized and ready to push versus when they feel the need for a lighter day or complete rest.
- Adapt Training Loads: Be flexible in adjusting training loads based on the athlete's ongoing feedback, competition schedules, and signs of overtraining. It's not about sticking rigidly to a plan but adapting it to the athlete's current needs.
- Scheduled Rest Days: Incorporate scheduled rest days into training plans. These should be days where physical activity is minimal, allowing for complete physical and mental recovery.
- Monitor and Adjust: Regularly review and adjust training plans based on performance, signs of overtraining, and the athlete's feedback. This might mean increasing rest days, adjusting training intensity, or altering focus areas in response to the athlete's progress and well-being.

In weaving rest and recovery into the fabric of a young baseball player's routine, we provide them with the tools not just to succeed but to thrive. It ensures they can bring their best selves to every practice, every game, and every challenge, both on and off the field. Through rest, we offer them a foundation for sustainable growth, peak performance, and a love for the game that burns brightly without burning out.

3.9 BALANCING BASEBALL WITH SCHOOL AND SOCIAL LIFE

For young athletes, the dream of excelling in baseball often comes with the reality of juggling schoolwork and maintaining an active social life. This balancing act, while challenging, is not insurmountable. With the right strategies and support, players can thrive both on the field and off, ensuring a well-rounded experience that enriches their lives in multiple dimensions.

Navigating the demands of being a young athlete requires a thoughtful approach to time management, setting priorities, and leaning on a supportive network of family, friends, and teammates. The goal is to cultivate a lifestyle that allows for passion, achievement, and joy in all areas of life.

Challenges of Balancing Commitments

Young players often feel the weight of their commitments pulling them in different directions. School assignments, baseball practice, games, and spending time with friends and family can feel like competing interests, each demanding time and energy. Recognizing this struggle is the first step in managing it effectively. It's about finding harmony among these aspects, not choosing one over the others.

Time Management Strategies

Effective time management is crucial for young athletes trying to balance their commitments. Here are a few strategies that can help:

- Plan Ahead: Use a planner or digital app to schedule schoolwork, practices, games, and social activities. Seeing everything laid out can help identify potential conflicts or crunch times, allowing for adjustments before they become stressful.
- Prioritize Tasks: Not all tasks are created equal. Identifying which assignments or activities are most urgent or important can help determine where to focus energy first.
- Use Downtime Wisely: Short periods between activities can be perfect for squeezing in study sessions or relaxation. Even a 15-minute review of notes between practice and dinner can make a difference.
- Stay Organized: Keeping track of assignments, practice schedules, and social commitments can reduce the feeling of being overwhelmed. A tidy workspace and organized sports gear can also save time and reduce stress.

Setting Priorities

Understanding what's truly important can help young athletes make decisions that align with their goals and well-being. Here's how they can set and adjust their priorities:

- Reflect on Goals: Regularly taking stock of what they want to achieve in baseball, school, and their personal lives can help athletes align their daily actions with their long-term objectives.
- Be Flexible: Priorities can shift, and that's okay. What's important one month might change the next. Being open to reassessing and adjusting priorities ensures that athletes are always working towards what matters most to them at any given time.
- Learn to Say No: Not every social invitation or extra baseball clinic must be accepted. Learning to say no to things that don't align with their current priorities can free up time for what truly matters.

The Role of Support Systems

Having a strong support system is invaluable for young athletes striving to balance their commitments. Here's why:

- Family Support: Parents and siblings can offer practical help, like transportation to practices or help with homework, and emotional support, offering encouragement and a listening ear when challenges arise.
- Friends Outside of Baseball: Maintaining friendships outside of the team provides a valuable outlet for relaxation and a reminder that there's life beyond baseball.
- Teammates as Allies: Teammates who share the experience of balancing sports and life can offer tips, share in the struggles, and celebrate the victories, both big and small.

- Coaches and Teachers: Open communication with coaches and teachers can lead to understanding and accommodations when schedules conflict or when extra support is needed.

In navigating the complexities of school, baseball, and social life, young athletes learn invaluable lessons in time management, setting priorities, and leaning on others for support. These skills, developed on the backdrop of their sports commitments, prepare them for the challenges and opportunities that lie ahead, in baseball and beyond.

As we wrap up this exploration into balancing commitments, it's clear that the journey of a young athlete is about much more than just sports. It's a holistic experience that encompasses personal growth, academic achievements, and meaningful relationships. By adopting effective time management strategies, setting and adjusting priorities based on evolving goals, and relying on a supportive network, young players set themselves up for success in all areas of their lives. This balanced approach not only enhances their baseball performance but also enriches their overall experience, ensuring they grow not just as athletes, but as individuals.

As we turn our attention to the next chapter, we'll continue to build on these foundational skills, exploring new strategies and insights that support young athletes in their pursuit of excellence, on the field and off.

CHAPTER 4
ELEVATING YOUR GAME

"My motto was always to keep swinging. Whether I was in a slump or feeling bad or having trouble off the field, the only thing to do was keep swinging." – Hank Aaron

Imagine stepping into a batting cage, not just to swing but to revolutionize how you hit. This chapter isn't about the basics; it's about tweaking, refining, and pushing beyond what you thought possible in your batting technique. It's about turning every at-bat into an opportunity to demonstrate power and precision.

4.1 ADVANCED BATTING TECHNIQUES: POWER AND PLACEMENT

The Science of Hitting

Hitting a baseball is often compared to the precision required to thread a needle. It's about aligning numerous elements perfectly, from the stance to the swing's follow-through. The biomechanics of a powerful hit start with leveraging body weight and rotational force. Here's how:

- Stance: It all begins here. A slightly wider stance can offer a stable base. Think of it as setting up the foundation of a building; the stronger the base, the taller and more stable the structure.

- Hip Rotation: Power in hitting doesn't come from the arms; it's generated from the hips. Rotating your hips before making contact with the ball can significantly increase the power behind your swing.

- Follow Through: The motion shouldn't stop at contact. Continuing the swing through the ball ensures that all the power generated from your body is transferred to the ball.

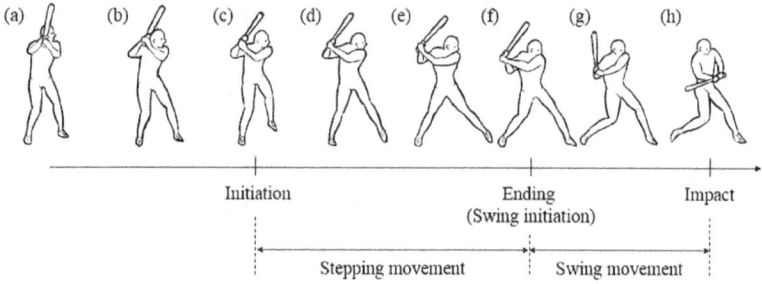

Mastering Bat Control

Precision in placing hits can often outshine sheer power. It's about making the ball go where you want it to. Here are strategies to improve bat control:

- Soft Toss Drills: Practicing with soft tosses can help refine your ability to direct the ball. Try aiming for different parts of the field, visualizing where you want the ball to land as you hit.

- Tee Work: Hitting off a tee isn't just for beginners. Adjusting the tee's height and location can help practice hitting balls in various strike zones, enhancing control over ball placement.

Power Hitting Drills

Incorporating specific drills into your practice sessions can significantly increase your bat speed and power. Focus on drills that emphasize core strength and hand-eye coordination, such as:

- Medicine Ball Throws: These can enhance core strength, crucial for powerful swings. Try rotational throws against a wall to mimic the hip rotation in your swing.
- Speed Swings: Using a lighter bat, perform swings focusing purely on speed. This can help improve the quick-twitch muscle fibers involved in swinging, leading to faster, more powerful hits.

Adjusting for Pitch Types

Every pitcher has a unique arsenal, and adapting your swing for different pitches can keep you a step ahead. Here's how:

- Fastballs: Timing is critical. Practice your swing timing with a pitching machine set to faster speeds to get used to making contact with fastballs.
- Curveballs and Sliders: These pitches can be deceptive. Focus on recognizing the pitch as early as possible and adjust your swing timing accordingly. Patience is key; let the ball come to you.

Incorporating these advanced techniques into your practice routines can significantly impact your performance at the plate. It's all about the details; fine-tuning your stance, mastering your swing mechanics, and learning to read pitches better will elevate your hitting game to new heights. Remember, great hitters are made in the cage and on the practice field, one swing at a time.

Strengthening your hitting game requires patience, persistence, and a willingness to delve into the nuances of batting mechanics. It's about more than just swinging harder; it's about swinging smarter, with intention and precision. With these advanced techniques and focused practice, you'll not only hit the ball harder but also place it exactly where you want, challenging defenses and changing the course of games.

4.2 PITCHING MECHANICS: DEVELOPING A KILLER PITCH

The craft of pitching goes far beyond simply throwing a baseball. It is an intricate dance of power, precision, and mental acuity, each element playing a critical role in outsmarting the batter. To elevate your game from good to exceptional, it's vital to expand your arsenal with advanced pitching techniques, adopt a strategic mindset, prioritize arm care, and learn the subtle art of controlling the game from the mound.

Advanced Pitching Techniques

Expanding your pitching repertoire is like adding more tools to your toolbox. Each new pitch offers a unique way to challenge and confuse batters, making you a more versatile and formidable pitcher.

- Slider: This pitch combines the speed of a fastball with the lateral movement of a curveball. The key is in the grip and the wrist action, which requires snapping the wrist at the point of release to impart the right spin.
- Curveball: Mastery of the curveball starts with the grip. Holding the ball with the index and middle finger along the seam, you'll create a downward spin that makes the ball "drop" as it approaches the plate, deceiving the batter.
- Changeup: The changeup is all about deception. With the same arm action as a fastball, changing the grip to reduce the pitch's velocity without altering your motion keeps batters off balance.

Integrating these pitches into your game involves practice and an understanding of when to use each for maximum effect. For example, a well-timed changeup can be devastating after a series of fastballs, catching the batter on their front foot and leading to an easy out.

Pitching 101

There are many variations thrown in the major leagues, but these eight pitches form the foundation.

Four-seam fastball

ALSO KNOWN AS: (General fastball terms) heater, cheese, smoke, cheddar, big dog
AVERAGE SPEED: 89-91 mph
WHICH MARINERS THROW IT: All
BEST IN THE AMERICAN LEAGUE* (ALL FASTBALLS): Pedro Martinez, Boston; Troy Percival, Anaheim; Bartolo Colon, Cleveland

WHAT IT DOES: The most basic, fundamental pitch, this is the only one thrown by everyone. It is the easiest pitch to locate (put it where you want it). The four-seamer is thrown at maximum velocity, with the ball coming off the first two fingers and rotating from top (6 to 12 on a clock) as viewed by the batter. It gets its name from the way the four parallel seams spin toward the batter, and that's what the batter is looking for to identify it.

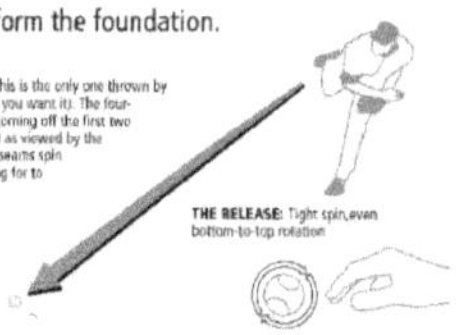

THE RELEASE: Tight spin, even bottom-to-top rotation

> "Every batter has nightmares about catching a fastball between the eyes. Stare at him and plant that dream in his head. Make him afraid, and he's half invisible already."
>
> John Sayles, "Pride of the Bimbos"

Two-seam fastball

ALSO KNOWN AS: Sinker
AVERAGE SPEED: 89-91 mph
WHICH MARINERS THROW IT: Abbott, Halama, Moyer, Paniagua and Sele (throw mostly two-seamers. Everyone else except Rhodes throws it with varying frequency.

WHAT IT DOES: For the two-seamer, the first and second fingers lay across the narrow area between the two horseshoe-shaped seam outlines. It is released the same way as the four-seamer, but the slight difference in the pronation of the hand causes it to rotate off-center, where a four-seamer rotates 6-to-12 on a clock face in the batter's view, a two-seamer still rotates but might be 4-to-10. That causes the ball to sink to some degree, though this is not considered a "breaking pitch" and is thrown at full velocity. It's called the two-seamer because, due to the grip, the batter sees only one pair or horizontal seams spinning, instead of two. This pitch is slightly more difficult to locate than the four-seamer, but still is thrown with good control.

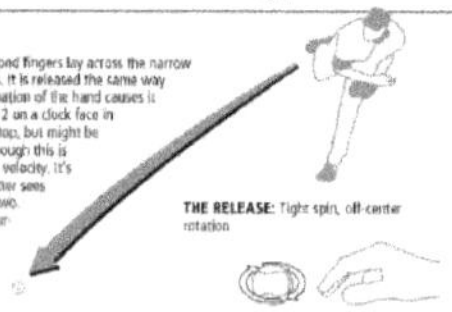

THE RELEASE: Tight spin, off-center rotation

> "The power pitcher — the man who can rear back and fog it by the hitter — is the brightest star in the pitching firmament."
>
> John Thorn and John Holway, "The Pitcher"

Changeup

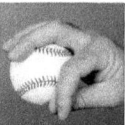

ALSO KNOWN AS: Off-speed pitch, dead fish, Peggy Lee, shirt, horseshoe
AVERAGE SPEED: 7-11 mph slower than fastball
WHICH MARINERS THROW IT: Abbott, Franklin, Garcia, Halama, Moyer, Pineiro, Rhodes, Sele
BEST IN THE LEAGUE*: Pedro Martinez, Boston; Brad Radke, Minnesota; Jamie Moyer, Mariners

WHAT IT DOES: The changeup is the great impostor, meant to look like the fastball, but coming in slower to throw off the batter's timing. The arm motion and release point are ideally the same as the fastball, but the difference is the grip. The most common grip is some form of the "circle change," in which the thumb and forefinger touch to create a circle on the side of the ball, which sits back close to the palm. The remaining fingers are spread around the ball. Where the fastball uses leverage to impart force and spin using the first two fingers, the changeup spreads the force around the ball, concentrating it in the middle of the ball and taking speed off. Variations on the grip include the palm ball, where the ball is held all the way back in the palm, and the horseshoe or pitchfork change, in which fingers are spread evenly around the ball, without the thumb-and-forefinger circle.

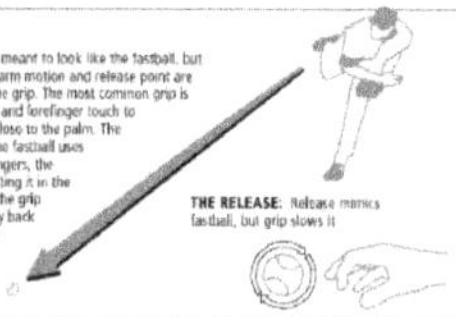

THE RELEASE: Release mimics fastball, but grip slows it

> "Hitting is timing. Pitching is upsetting timing."
>
> Warren Spahn, legendary HOF pitcher

Curveball

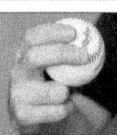

ALSO KNOWN AS: Hammer, yellow hammer, whip, yakker
AVERAGE SPEED: 11-14 mph slower than fastball
WHICH MARINERS THROW IT: Garcia, Halama, Pineiro, Sasaki, Sele. Moyer and Abbott have the pitch, but generally throw fewer than five per game.
BEST IN THE LEAGUE*: Mike Mussina, New York; Aaron Sele, Mariners; Troy Percival, Anaheim

WHAT IT DOES: The curve is unusual in that it rotates from top to bottom, rather than from bottom to top like the fastball. That's because instead of being released forward, in the direction of the fingers toward the batter, the curve is thrown with the wrist cocked so that the thumb is on top. With the arm coming down, the ball rolls over the outside of the index finger, causing a downward spin. The curve sinks dramatically and can be thrown for a strike or a "miss" pitch. Depending on the arm position of the individual pitcher — straight over the top or more sidearm — the ball might also break across the plate and wind up outside. On this pitch, having the hand speed to transfer leverage to the front of the ball is more important than arm strength.

THE RELEASE: Ball tumbles over index finger, opposite rotation from fastball

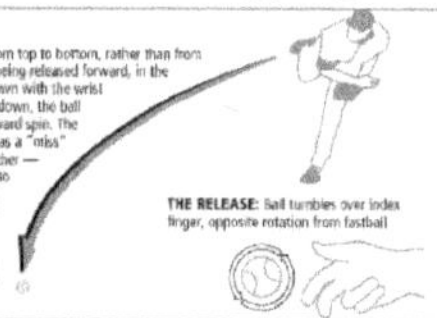

> "In the confrontation between batter and pitcher, it is the curveball that makes the batter the underdog."
>
> Martin Quigley, "The Crooked Pitch"

Slider

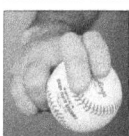

ALSO KNOWN AS: No common nickname
AVERAGE SPEED: 4-6 mph slower than fastball
WHICH MARINERS THROW IT: Abbott, Charlton, Franklin, Halama, Nelson, Paniagua, Pineiro, Rhodes
BEST IN THE LEAGUE*: Jeff Nelson, Mariners; Pedro Martinez, Boston; Tim Hudson, Oakland

WHAT IT DOES: The slider is the next-fastest pitch to the fastball, and it relies on a tight spin that mimics the fastball, plus a pronounced late break down and away (in a righty-vs.-righty matchup). The grip has the first two fingers close together and off-center, positioned above the length of a seam. On release, the pitcher uses the contact along the length of the seam and pulls downward to create spin. The slider uses the leverage of the seam, rather than a wrist action, to impart spin: try to do both at the same time and you're headed for arm problems. The spin is not straight through the ball, but off-center, due to the grip, and that spin pattern eventually causes the ball to "snap off" at a downward angle as it approaches the plate. The speed is below that of the fastball, but the closer a pitcher can get to throwing it at fastball speed, the better.

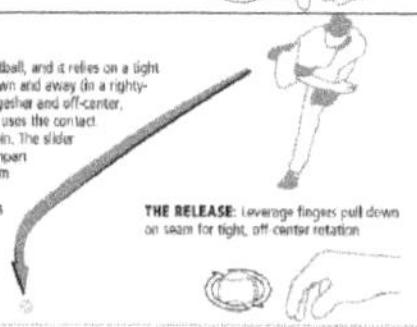

THE RELEASE: Leverage fingers pull down on seam for tight, off-center rotation

> "It is the pitch that has changed the game of baseball... You can see the spin, but unless you anticipate it or the pitcher hangs it, there is not much chance of your hitting it solidly."
>
> Lou Piniella, Mariners manager

Split-finger

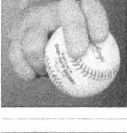

ALSO KNOWN AS: Splitter
AVERAGE SPEED: 4-6 mph slower than fastball
WHICH MARINERS THROW IT: Franklin, Paniagua
BEST IN THE LEAGUE*: Tim Hudson, Oakland

WHAT IT DOES: The splitter comes in with tight rotation and good velocity and dives straight down at the last second. The grip is similar to the two-seam fastball, but with the fingers spread farther apart to change the rotation and add break. This pitch is generally not thrown for strikes, but to coax a swing and miss.

THE RELEASE: Same as fastball

> "The key to an effective split-finger is to think fastball."
>
> Roger Craig, former pitcher/coach

Forkball

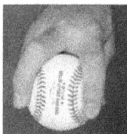

ALSO KNOWN AS: Fork
AVERAGE SPEED: Varies, as fast as 84-86 mph but usually slower
WHICH MARINERS THROW IT: Sasaki, Charlton and, rarely, Nelson
BEST IN THE LEAGUE*: Kazuhiro Sasaki, Seattle; Roger Clemens, New York

WHAT IT DOES: For the fork, take the split-finger grip and spread the fingers out as far as possible so that they are almost at the sides of the ball, and the ball sits back more toward the palm. The pitch was allegedly invented by Dave Keefe, a pitcher from 1917-22 who held the ball between his index and fourth fingers because he had lost the middle finger in a childhood accident. This grip takes a lot of velocity off the ball but causes an extreme break. Like the splitter, the fork is not thrown for strikes and usually winds up in the dirt. But if you can get a batter to commit his swing when it looks like it's headed for the strike zone, by the time the bat gets there, the ball's underneath it. This one can make a batter look very bad.

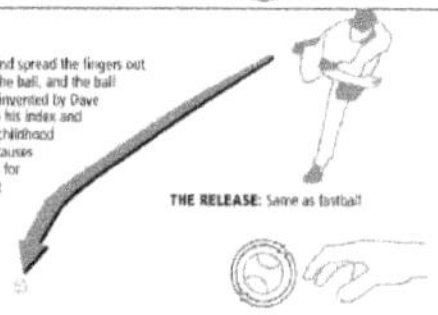

THE RELEASE: Same as fastball

> "If you throw a 97-mph fastball, then come back with a 87-mph forkball, the hitter sees the same as it each time. Not only could he end up out front of the ball (swinging early), he could be swinging at a ball that has just plunged into the dirt."
>
> Roger Clemens, Yankees pitcher

Knuckleball

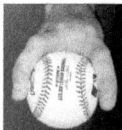

ALSO KNOWN AS: Knuckler, dancer, various expletives
AVERAGE SPEED: Anywhere from 50s to 70s
WHICH MARINERS THROW IT: None
BEST IN THE LEAGUE*: Boston's Tim Wakefield is the most effective knuckleballer of his generation. Detroit's Steve Sparks is the only other AL knuckleball starter.

WHAT IT DOES: The knuckle is rare, difficult to learn, difficult to control and even more difficult to hit. Gripped with the tips of the first two fingers on top and anchored at the bottom by the thumb, the knuckleball is pushed straight out at the release. There is ideally no spin at all, and the air moving against the seams pushes the ball around at its will.
Knuckleball pitchers throw the pitch almost exclusively, but usually mix in a fastball. Hitters hate the knuckler because it is so slow it's difficult to time, and even if you know what it's going to get there, there's no way to predict where it's going to be. Dick Allen, a star first baseman in the '60s and '70s, said the safest thing was to take your three swings and sit down: "I'm afraid if I even think about hitting it, I'll mess up my swing for life."

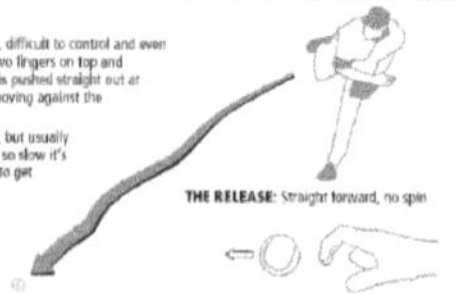

THE RELEASE: Straight forward, no spin

> "Like some cult religion that barely survives, there has always been at least one bad rarely more than five or six devotees throwing the knuckleball in the big leagues ... Not only can't pitchers control it, hitters can't hit it, catchers can't catch it, coaches can't coach it, and most pitchers can't stand it. The perfect pitch."
>
> Ron Luciano, former AL umpire

Pitching Strategy

The mental game is as crucial as physical skill in pitching. Developing a pitching strategy involves understanding batters' weaknesses, setting up pitches, and making intelligent pitch selections based on the game situation.

- Reading Batters: Pay attention to batters' stances, swings, and habits. A batter crowding the plate might struggle with inside pitches, while one standing back may have difficulty reaching outside pitches.
- Setting Up Pitches: Use your pitches strategically to set up batters. For instance, a series of fastballs can make a well-placed curveball more effective by disrupting the batter's timing.
- Strategic Pitch Selection: Consider the count, the number of outs, and base runners when choosing your pitch. A fastball might be the safest choice when behind in the count, while an off-speed pitch could surprise a batter expecting a fastball in a hitters' count.

Arm Care and Conditioning

Taking care of your arm is non-negotiable. A healthy arm is your most valuable asset as a pitcher, so prioritizing arm care through conditioning, proper mechanics, and rest is essential to a long and successful pitching career.

- Strengthening Exercises: Focus on exercises that strengthen the shoulder, elbow, and forearm muscles. Resistance bands and light dumbbell exercises can build strength without adding unnecessary strain.

- Proper Mechanics: Adhering to proper pitching mechanics not only improves efficiency and power but also reduces the risk of injury. Ensure your pitching motion is smooth and consistent, avoiding any unnecessary strain on your arm.
- Rest and Recovery: Adequate rest between pitching sessions is crucial. Following pitch count guidelines and ensuring sufficient days off between appearances protects your arm from overuse injuries.

Controlling the Game

A pitcher who can control the game dictates the pace and keeps batters and base runners off balance. This control is achieved through tempo, pick-off moves, and maintaining composure under pressure.

- Tempo: Establish a rhythm that keeps your defense alert and ready, but don't be so predictable that batters can time you easily. Varying your tempo can disrupt a batter's timing.
- Pick-Off Moves: A well-executed pick-off move not only has the potential to get an out but also keeps base runners close to the bag, making it harder for them to steal.
- Composure: Perhaps the most crucial aspect of controlling the game is maintaining your composure, especially in high-pressure situations. Breathe, focus on one pitch at a time, and trust your training and abilities.

Developing as a pitcher involves more than just throwing harder; it's about thinking smarter, caring for your body, and becoming a master of the game within the game. With dedication to refining your pitching techniques, adopting a strategic approach, prioritizing arm health, and learning to control the game's pace, you'll not only elevate your pitching game but also become an invaluable asset to your team.

4.3 CATCHING TECHNIQUES: MASTERING THE ART OF FRAMING

Behind every great pitcher stands a catcher whose role far exceeds merely catching pitches. This position, pivotal in baseball, demands a blend of physical agility, sharp mental acumen, and an almost telepathic connection with the pitcher. The catcher is the field general, orchestrating the game's flow, strategizing pitch sequences, and fortifying the team's defense.

The Role of the Catcher

The catcher's influence spans the entirety of the game, touching on every pitch, every out, and every inning. Adept at reading the game's nuances, catchers call pitches, making split-second decisions that can alter the game's outcome. They are the pitcher's closest ally, offering reassurance, strategizing pitch selection, and, when necessary, stepping in to recalibrate a pitcher's focus. Beyond this, catchers coordinate the defense, positioning fielders to best counter the batter's tendencies.

Framing Techniques

The subtle art of framing can sway an umpire's call, turning a borderline pitch into a strike. Mastery in framing hinges on a few key techniques:

- Steady Hands: A catcher's glove movement at the moment of catching the pitch can influence an umpire's perception. Keeping the glove steady and making minimal, precise movements can make a pitch appear more accurate.

- Body Positioning: Aligning your body to present the pitch as within the strike zone, regardless of its actual path, can subtly influence the umpire's call. This requires not just skill but an understanding of each umpire's strike zone tendencies.

- Glove Movement: A slight turn of the wrist to bring the glove back into the strike zone, known as "bringing the pitch back," can be effective when done subtly. Overdoing this movement, however, can have the opposite effect, drawing attention to the pitch's initial placement outside the strike zone.

Blocking and Throw-Downs

A catcher's defensive capabilities are tested in their ability to block wild pitches and execute quick, accurate throws to bases. Here's how they can hone these skills:

- Blocking Techniques: Anticipating a pitch's path and using your body as a barrier to keep the ball in front of you is crucial. This requires not just quick reflexes but also the courage to face a fast-moving ball head-on.

- Throw-Downs: The ability to throw a runner out hinges on a quick, fluid transition from catching to throwing. Practicing footwork and throw mechanics can shave precious milliseconds off your throw, making the difference in tight situations.

Catcher-Pitcher Communication

The relationship between a catcher and their pitcher is foundational to a team's success. Clear, concise signals that leave no room for doubt are the bedrock of this partnership. But communication extends beyond just signs:

- Pitch Selection: A catcher must understand a pitcher's strengths, weaknesses, and mental state to call the game effectively. This involves knowing when to push for a challenging pitch and when to rely on the pitcher's comfort pitches.
- Managing Pitcher Psychology: Catchers often act as psychologists, reading the pitcher's mood and confidence levels. They must know when to offer encouragement, when to call time for a brief chat, and when to let a pitcher work through their challenges independently.

In mastering these techniques, catchers elevate their game, becoming indispensable assets to their team. They not only safeguard the plate but also enhance the pitcher's performance, direct the team's defense, and subtly influence the game's flow. This comprehensive skill set makes the catcher's role both demanding and rewarding, demanding constant learning, adaptation, and mental fortitude.

The catcher's journey is one of continuous growth, seeking not just to react to the game but to anticipate and shape its course. With every pitch, every out, and every game, catchers have the opportunity to refine their skills, deepen their understanding of the game, and reinforce their position as pivotal players on the field. In doing so, they not only contribute to their team's success but also to the rich, complex tapestry of baseball itself.

4.4 BASE STEALING SECRETS: THE ART OF THE STEAL

Stealing bases in baseball is much like a magician executing a perfect illusion; it requires timing, skill, and a bit of daring. This segment of our exploration focuses on turning players into adept base stealers, capable of taking extra bases and applying pressure on the opposing team's defense and pitching staff. Mastering this aspect of the game not only enhances a player's value but also adds an exciting dynamic to their team's offensive strategy.

Timing and Technique

The foundation of successful base stealing lies in mastering the timing and developing the right technique. Here's how to refine these crucial aspects:

- Study Pitchers' Movements: Observing and understanding pitchers' habits and delivery times to the plate are critical. Look for patterns or tells that indicate when they're about to pitch.
- Lead and Jump: Work on taking a lead that's aggressive yet safe. As for the jump, it's all about the first step. Practice short, explosive bursts of speed the moment you decide to steal, aiming to minimize reaction time.

- Secondary Leads: Enhance your ability to take secondary leads. A well-timed bounce as the pitcher commits to the plate can give you the extra momentum needed for a successful steal.

Psychology of Stealing Bases

Intimidation plays a significant role in the art of the steal. A base stealer who can get into the heads of pitchers and catchers has already won half the battle. Here are ways to cultivate this psychological edge:

- Non-Verbal Cues: Use body language to project confidence and intent. Even when not planning to steal, a convincing lead can distract and unsettle the pitcher.
- Aggressiveness: Consistently demonstrating a willingness to steal puts pressure on the pitcher, potentially leading to mistakes or advantageous pitches for your teammates.

Slide Techniques

Sliding is not just about reaching the base but doing so safely and effectively. Different situations call for different slides:

- Head-First Slide: Useful for avoiding tags and reaching distant parts of the base. Practice keeping your hands up to avoid injury and perfecting the timing to maintain speed while sliding.
- Pop-Up Slide: Ideal when you intend to take advantage of an overthrow or a missed catch. Work on transitioning from the slide back to a standing position quickly and efficiently.

- Hook Slide: Employ this slide to avoid tags by reaching around the tag with your hand. It's tricky but can be incredibly effective when done right.

Training for Speed and Agility

Speed and agility are the physical cornerstones of stealing bases. Incorporating specific exercises and drills into your training can significantly improve your stealing capabilities:

- Sprint Drills: Short sprints, especially those that mimic the distance between bases, can improve acceleration and speed.
- Agility Ladder Drills: These enhance footwork and agility, making it easier to change directions swiftly, an asset when avoiding tags.
- Plyometrics: Exercises like box jumps and squat jumps increase explosive power, directly translating to quicker jumps and faster sprints.
- Resistance Training: Using resistance bands or parachutes while sprinting can build strength in the muscles used during sprinting, enhancing overall speed.

Stealing bases is an art form that combines physical prowess, mental sharpness, and sheer audacity. Excelling in this aspect of the game requires diligent practice, keen observation, and the courage to take risks. By focusing on timing and technique, understanding the psychological warfare involved, mastering various slide techniques, and training specifically for speed and agility, players can become formidable base-stealing threats. This not only contributes to their personal arsenal of skills but also brings an invaluable dynamic to their team's offensive strategy, keeping opponents on their toes and creating opportunities to score.

4.5 IN-DEPTH FIELDING STRATEGIES: BEYOND THE BASICS

Fielding in baseball is akin to an intricate dance. Each step, each movement, must be precise, deliberate, and perfectly timed. This level of excellence in fielding doesn't just happen. It's the product of relentless practice, a deep understanding of the game, and an unyielding commitment to excellence. Let's explore how to elevate your fielding game, transforming you into the linchpin of your team's defense.

Advanced Positioning

Positioning on the field is not just about where you stand; it's about anticipating where the ball will be hit and being there before it arrives. This premeditated placement relies on a variety of factors:

- Batter Tendencies: Pay close attention to batters' histories and their tendencies. A pull-hitter, for instance, is likely to send the ball to the opposite field, demanding a shift in your positioning.
- Pitcher's Arsenal: The type of pitch being thrown significantly influences where the ball is likely to be hit. Fastballs might lead to late swings, suggesting a strategic shift towards the opposite field.
- Situational Awareness: The game's context—number of outs, runners on base—should also dictate your

positioning. With a runner on first, positioning yourself to cover a potential double play becomes crucial.

Handling Difficult Plays

The mark of a great fielder is not just making routine plays but also pulling off the seemingly impossible ones. Here are techniques to master some of the most challenging plays in baseball:

- Diving Catches: Perfecting a diving catch requires not just bravery but also technique. Practice diving forward and to the side, keeping your eye on the ball until it hits your glove. It's about commitment; hesitate, and you've already missed the catch.
- Wall Plays: Fielding balls near the wall demands spatial awareness. Practice backpedaling to the wall during drills, using your non-glove hand to feel for the wall, allowing you to focus your eyes on the ball.
- Over-the-Shoulder Catches: These are particularly tricky but can be mastered with the right approach. Running with your back to the infield, practice locating the ball over your shoulder, using quick glances to adjust your path as you run.

Double Play Mechanics

The double play is one of baseball's most exhilarating moments, requiring seamless coordination and flawless execution. Here's how different positions can work together to turn two:

- Middle Infielders: The key here is the quick transfer of the ball from glove to hand. Practice this transfer relentlessly, focusing on fluid motions that eliminate any wasted time.

- First Basemen: Position yourself to provide a clear target for the throw, stretching towards the incoming ball to shorten the distance it needs to travel.

- Third Basemen and Pitchers: When involved in a double play, your throw to second needs to be precise. Aim for the chest area to ensure a smooth catch and transfer for the middle infielders.

Fielding as Game Strategy

Fielding is not just about stopping hits; it's a strategic tool that can shift the momentum of the game. Here's how to leverage your fielding skills strategically:

- Infield In: In situations where a ground ball could allow a runner from third to score, pulling the infield in can prevent this run, though it comes with the risk of allowing hits through the infield.

- Shifts: Implementing shifts based on batter tendencies can frustrate hitters and force them into making uncomfortable adjustments to their approach.

- Communication: Loud, clear communication between fielders can turn potential collisions into smooth outs. Practice calling for balls with authority, ensuring your teammates know to defer to your call.

Each of these strategies, techniques, and approaches to fielding is about more than just stopping the ball. They're about understanding the game on a deeper level, anticipating actions before they happen, and positioning yourself not just as a defender but as a strategist. It's this mindset, this dedication to the craft of fielding, that transforms good fielders into great ones. By focusing on advanced positioning, mastering the art of making difficult plays, understanding the mechanics behind successful double plays, and viewing fielding as an integral part of your team's strategy, you elevate not just your game but your team's chances of success.

4.6 MENTAL STRATEGIES FOR COMPETITIVE PLAY

In the heat of competition, where every pitch, hit, and play carries the weight of expectation, the mental aspect of baseball becomes as crucial as the physical. Players who can harness their mental faculties, control their emotions, and visualize success often find themselves performing at their peak, even under immense pressure. This section delves into the mental strategies that can elevate a player's game, offering tools for sharpening game intelligence, maintaining emotional equilibrium, harnessing the power of visualization, and learning from the best to inspire growth and resilience.

Game Intelligence

Understanding the game at a deeper level allows players to anticipate outcomes, make informed decisions quickly, and adapt to changing situations on the field. Enhancing game intelligence involves:

- Study the Game: Dedicate time to learning the nuances of baseball, including rules, strategies, and positions. Knowledge is power, and a deep understanding of the game can give you a strategic advantage.

- Analyze Situations: Regularly put yourself in hypothetical game situations during practice. Ask yourself, "What would I do if...?" This mental exercise sharpens decision-making skills and prepares you for real-game scenarios.

- Learn From Each Play: After each game, take time to reflect on key moments. What worked? What didn't? This reflection turns experience into wisdom, contributing to your overall game intelligence.

Emotional Control

The ability to stay calm and focused under pressure is what often separates the good from the great. Developing techniques for emotional control is essential:

- Breathing Techniques: Practice deep, controlled breathing to help calm your nerves before and during games. A simple technique is the 4-7-8 method: inhale for 4 seconds, hold for 7, and exhale for 8. This helps reduce anxiety and maintain focus.

- Mental Rehearsal: Before games, spend a few minutes visualizing yourself handling high-pressure situations with calm and grace. Imagining success can boost confidence and reduce game-day jitters.

- Stay Present: Concentrate on the here and now, not past mistakes or future plays. Mindfulness exercises can help you stay focused on the current moment, enhancing performance and emotional control.

Visualization for Advanced Play

Visualization, or mental rehearsal, is a powerful tool for athletes, allowing them to experience success before stepping onto the field. To utilize visualization for advanced play:

- Create Detailed Scenarios: Visualize specific game situations, from standing at the plate to making a game-saving catch. The more detailed the scenario, the more effective the visualization.
- Engage All Senses: Incorporate all your senses into the visualization. What does the bat feel like in your hands? How does the grass smell? Engaging your senses makes the visualization more realistic and impactful.
- Positive Outcomes Only: Focus on visualizing positive outcomes. Seeing yourself succeed in your mind's eye can boost confidence and reinforce muscle memory, translating to better performance on the field.

Learning from the Pros

Observing and learning from professional players can offer invaluable insights into the mental approaches and strategies that contribute to their success. Here's how to make the most of this resource:

- Watch Games with a Critical Eye: Instead of just enjoying the game, analyze the decisions and moves of professional players. Why did they choose that pitch? What positioning did the fielder take, and why?
- Interviews and Autobiographies: Many professional players share their experiences, challenges, and mental strategies in interviews and autobiographies. These can be goldmines of inspiration and practical advice.
- Mimic Mental Routines: Many pros have pre-game rituals and mental routines they follow to prepare for competition. Experiment with adopting similar routines to see what works best for you, customizing them to fit your style and needs.

Incorporating these mental strategies into your repertoire can profoundly impact your approach to the game. By honing your game intelligence, you're better equipped to make split-second decisions that can change the course of a game. Through emotional control, you remain calm and focused, even when the stakes are high. Visualization practices enable you to mentally rehearse success, building confidence and reinforcing positive outcomes. Lastly, learning from professional players offers a roadmap to developing a resilient, strategic approach to baseball, inspiring you to continuously evolve and improve your mental game.

4.7 LEADERSHIP ON AND OFF THE FIELD: BEING A TEAM CAPTAIN

Qualities of a Leader

In the heart of a team captain lies a myriad of qualities that do more than just lead; they inspire, motivate, and elevate the team's spirit. A captain's role extends beyond just strategy and gameplay; it's about embodying the essence of teamwork and sportsmanship. Here are the core qualities that make a great team leader:

- Communication: Clear, effective communication is the cornerstone of leadership. It involves not just talking but listening, ensuring every team member feels heard and valued.

- Empathy: Understanding and sharing the feelings of teammates is crucial. It helps in forging strong connections, making it easier to support one another through ups and downs.

- Inspiration: The ability to inspire comes from leading by example, showing dedication, resilience, and passion for the game, which in turn motivates others to give their best.

- Decision-Making: A captain often needs to make quick decisions, whether it's on the field or off. Weighing options and choosing the best course of action for the team is a testament to a leader's judgment and wisdom.

Responsibilities of a Captain

The captaincy comes with a set of responsibilities that form the backbone of the team's structure and morale. These responsibilities are what set a captain apart, showcasing their commitment to the team's success:

- Representing the Team: As the face of the team, a captain represents their teammates in discussions with coaches, umpires, and even the media, ensuring the team's voice is heard and respected.
- Mediating Conflicts: Disagreements and conflicts are part and parcel of any team dynamic. A captain steps in to mediate these situations, finding solutions that are in the best interest of the team.
- Setting Goals: Goal setting is not just for personal improvement but for the team's growth. A captain works with teammates to set achievable goals, creating a roadmap for success.
- Fostering Unity: A team's strength lies in its unity. Encouraging teamwork, organizing team-building activities, and ensuring every player feels included are key responsibilities of a captain.

Leading by Example

The most profound impact a captain can have is through their actions. Leading by example is about embodying the values and work ethic you wish to see in your teammates:

- Work Ethic: Dedication to training, punctuality, and a never-give-up attitude are traits that inspire teammates to adopt the same level of commitment.

- Attitude: Maintaining a positive attitude, even in the face of defeat, sets a tone of resilience and optimism within the team.

- Sportsmanship: Showing respect for opponents, umpires, and the game itself teaches teammates the importance of integrity and fairness.

Developing Leadership Skills

Leadership is a skill that can be honed and developed over time. For those aspiring to be effective team captains, here are strategies to cultivate leadership qualities:

- Effective Communication: Practice active listening, where you give full attention to the speaker, and work on conveying your thoughts clearly and respectfully. Role-playing different scenarios with friends or family can help refine your communication skills.

- Motivating Teammates: Learn what motivates your teammates individually and as a group. This could be through recognizing achievements, offering encouragement, or simply knowing when a teammate needs a boost.

- Setting Goals: Practice setting SMART (Specific, Measurable, Achievable, Relevant, Time-bound) goals for yourself and learn how to guide others in setting their own. This can start with small, personal goals, gradually expanding to team objectives.

- Conflict Resolution: Develop mediation skills by learning conflict resolution techniques. Understanding how to navigate disagreements and find common ground is crucial in maintaining team harmony.

- Seek Feedback: Don't shy away from asking for feedback on your leadership style. Understanding how your actions and decisions are perceived can offer valuable insights into areas for improvement.

In embracing these qualities and responsibilities, and committing to the continuous development of leadership skills, a team captain can profoundly influence their team's cohesion, performance, and overall experience. Leadership on and off the field is about more than guiding a team to victory; it's about nurturing an environment where every player feels valued, motivated, and part of something greater than themselves. It's in this space that teams find their true strength, pushing beyond limits and achieving greatness, together.

4.8 UNDERSTANDING AND ANALYZING BASEBALL STATISTICS

In the realm of baseball, numbers do much more than just tally scores and record outcomes. They weave intricate tales of strategy, skill, and the subtle nuances that distinguish a good player from a great one. This section peels back the layers of statistical analysis, illuminating its role in enhancing performance, crafting game strategies, and providing a deeper understanding of one's contributions to the team.

Statistical Analysis for Players

For players, the world of statistics opens up a treasure trove of insights into their performance. Here's a closer look:

- Identify Strengths and Weaknesses: By analyzing hitting averages or ERA (Earned Run Average), players can pinpoint areas of strength to leverage, as well as aspects of their game needing improvement.
- Progress Tracking: Regularly reviewing statistical data allows players to track their development over time, providing tangible evidence of their hard work paying off or highlighting areas that require more focused effort.
- Preparation for Opponents: Studying the statistics of upcoming opponents can offer strategic advantages, revealing potential weaknesses to exploit or strengths to counter.

Through this analytical lens, players gain a clearer perspective on their journey, transforming raw data into actionable insights that drive improvement and strategic advantage.

Advanced Metrics

The sophistication of baseball analytics has surged, giving rise to advanced metrics that offer a deeper dive into a player's contribution. Here are a few key ones:

- WAR (Wins Above Replacement): This comprehensive stat measures a player's value in terms of the number of wins they contribute to their team above what a replacement player would offer. It encompasses aspects of batting, fielding, and base running.

- OPS (On-base Plus Slugging): By combining on-base percentage (how often a player gets on base) with slugging percentage (how well they hit for power), OPS provides a snapshot of a player's offensive productivity.
- BABIP (Batting Average on Balls in Play): This metric helps determine how often a player gets a hit when the ball is in play, excluding home runs. It can be useful in assessing luck or skill factors in batting performance.

Understanding these metrics can profoundly impact how players and coaches evaluate performance, going beyond traditional stats to a more nuanced appreciation of a player's overall contributions.

Using Statistics for Strategy

Strategically applied, statistics can significantly influence game outcomes. Here's how:

- Lineup Construction: Analyzing on-base percentages alongside slugging percentages can guide the assembly of a batting order optimized for scoring runs.
- Defensive Positioning: Using hit charts and BABIP metrics, coaches can position fielders more effectively, anticipating the most likely locations of batted balls.
- Pitching Matchups: Leveraging statistics like OPS against left-handed versus right-handed pitchers can inform decisions on pitching matchups, maximizing the chances of outs.

In this way, statistics become a powerful tool in the strategic arsenal, guiding decisions that can tilt the game in one's favor.

Tools and Resources for Analysis

For players and coaches keen on integrating statistical analysis into their approach, numerous tools and resources are available:

- Software Solutions: Programs like Statcast and Rapsodo offer detailed analytics, from pitch spin rates to exit velocities, providing a granular view of performance aspects.

- Websites: Platforms such as Baseball-Reference and Fangraphs serve as repositories of both traditional and advanced metrics, offering user-friendly interfaces for delving into player and team statistics.

- Mobile Apps: Apps like GameChanger provide real-time tracking of stats during games, making it easier for players and coaches to analyze performance on the go.

Equipped with these tools, the baseball community is better positioned to harness the power of data, translating numbers into insights that drive success on the field.

In wrapping up this exploration into the world of baseball statistics, it's clear that numbers do far more than just keep score. They serve as a mirror, reflecting the multifaceted contributions of players, the strategic intricacies of the game, and the pathways to personal and team growth. By demystifying these metrics and embracing the tools available for analysis, players and coaches unlock new dimensions of understanding and strategy, setting the stage for enhanced performance and deeper engagement with the beautiful game of baseball.

As we transition from the analytical to the practical, the journey continues, always with an eye towards refinement, strategy, and the unyielding pursuit of excellence that defines the sport.

CHAPTER 5
GUIDING YOUNG PLAYERS

"Baseball is a simple game. If you have good players and if you keep them in the right frame of mind, then the manager is a success." – Sparky Anderson

Every coach remembers the first time they realized the impact of their words and actions on young players. It's a moment of revelation that coaching goes beyond teaching the game—it's about shaping experiences that last a lifetime. This chapter zeros in on the strategies that transform good practice sessions into great ones, where players not only hone their skills but also find joy in every swing, catch, and sprint.

5.1 CREATING EFFECTIVE PRACTICE PLANS

When planning practice sessions, think of yourself as a chef. Just as a chef combines ingredients to create a dish that's both nutritious and delicious, a coach blends skill development with fun to cook up practice sessions that players look forward to. Here's how:

- Balancing Skill Development and Fun: Picture a seesaw. On one side, you've got drills that sharpen skills; on the other, games that make players laugh and lose track of time. Your goal? Keep that seesaw balanced. It might be integrating a game of "baseball tag" to work on sprinting and agility or ending practice with a home run derby. The key is ensuring that while players are improving, they're also enjoying the process.

- Incorporating Varied Training Methods: Every player has a unique way of learning. Some might grasp concepts quickly through visual aids, like diagrams showing the mechanics of a swing. Others might benefit from kinesthetic learning, where they learn by doing. Mixing drills that cater to visual, auditory, and kinesthetic learners ensures that each player gets the chance to shine. For instance, use video analysis for visual learners, call out instructions during drills for auditory learners, and provide hands-on adjustments for kinesthetic learners.

- Adjusting Plans to Player Needs: One size doesn't fit all when it comes to practice plans. A beginner might need more time mastering the basics, while an advanced player could be ready for more nuanced strategies. Tailoring your sessions to meet players where they are supports their development at every stage. This means maybe spending the first part of practice on fundamentals for newer players, then breaking off into more specialized groups where veterans can tackle complex plays.

- Feedback and Positive Reinforcement: Imagine finishing a tough drill and the coach says, "Great hustle out there!" That's fuel. Feedback and positive reinforcement not only boost morale but also encourage players to keep pushing their limits. Make it specific. Instead of a generic "good job," try "I noticed how you kept your eye on the ball through that catch—well done!" It shows you're paying attention and value their efforts.

Visual Element: Practice Plan Template

A downloadable template that outlines a balanced practice session, including time allocations for warm-up, skill development, fun activities, and cool-down. The template also includes sections for tailored activities based on skill level and learning style preferences.

Interactive Element: Practice Reflection Worksheet

A worksheet that encourages players to reflect on their practice sessions, answering questions like:

- What skill do you feel you improved on today?
- What was the most enjoyable part of practice?
- Is there a drill you struggle with? How can we make it better for you?

This interactive tool fosters a two-way conversation between coaches and players, ensuring practice sessions are responsive to players' needs and preferences.

In essence, effective practice plans are the backbone of a team's development. They ensure that every player, regardless of their starting point, is given the opportunity to grow, improve, and most importantly, fall in love with the game. By balancing skill development with fun, employing varied training methods, adjusting plans to meet individual needs, and providing constructive feedback, coaches can create an environment where young players thrive. This approach not only enhances their skills on the field but also instills a sense of joy and accomplishment that they carry with them long after the game is over.

5.2 COMMUNICATION SKILLS FOR COACHES AND PARENTS

In the realm of youth baseball, the ability to communicate effectively is as vital as the skills displayed on the field. It's the glue that binds coaches, parents, and players, fostering a nurturing environment conducive to growth, learning, and enjoyment. Below, we explore the pillars of robust communication strategies that cater to a harmonious baseball experience.

Effective Communication Techniques

- Active Listening: It's about giving undivided attention to the speaker, validating their feelings, and understanding their perspective without immediately jumping to solutions. This approach encourages openness and trust.
- Clarity and Conciseness: Especially important when instructing young players. Instructions should be clear,

avoiding ambiguity. It's helpful to break down complex concepts into simpler, manageable pieces.

- Non-Verbal Cues: Body language speaks volumes. Maintaining eye contact, nodding, and leaning forward shows engagement and encourages players and parents to express themselves freely.

- Positive Language: Framing feedback positively can motivate and uplift. For instance, instead of highlighting what went wrong, focus on how to improve. "Next time, try keeping your eye on the ball till it meets the bat," instead of "You missed the ball because you weren't looking."

Addressing Concerns and Conflicts

- Create a Safe Space: Encourage an environment where players and parents feel comfortable voicing concerns without fear of judgment. This might mean setting aside specific times for open discussions or one-on-one meetings.

- Emphasize Common Goals: Remind all parties involved of the shared objective: the players' growth and enjoyment of the game. This perspective can diffuse tension and foster a collaborative approach to conflict resolution.

- Seek to Understand Before Being Understood: A principle that ensures all sides feel heard. It involves asking probing questions to get to the root of the concern and then addressing it with empathy and understanding.

- Solution-Oriented Approach: Once all perspectives are understood, work together to find a solution that respects everyone's input. This might involve compromise or finding creative alternatives that satisfy all parties.

Encouraging Open Dialogue

- Regular Check-Ins: Establish regular intervals for feedback, not just about baseball skills but also about the players' overall experience. This can be done through informal chats, feedback forms, or group discussions.
- Empower Players to Speak Up: Teach young athletes the importance of communication in a team setting. Encourage them to articulate their thoughts, feelings, and aspirations about their baseball journey.
- Parent-Coach-Player Meetings: Facilitate meetings that include the player, their parents, and the coach. This triad approach ensures everyone is on the same page regarding the player's development, both on and off the field.

Role Modeling Positive Communication

- Demonstrate Respectful Interactions: Coaches and parents are role models. Demonstrating respectful, constructive communication in every interaction sets a powerful example for young players.
- Admitting Mistakes: Showing that it's okay to make mistakes, as long as one learns from them, teaches valuable lessons in humility and growth. When coaches or parents mishandle a situation, owning up and discussing ways to improve models accountability and integrity.

- Celebrating Efforts and Achievements: Make it a habit to acknowledge and celebrate the efforts and achievements of players, no matter how small. This not only boosts morale but also reinforces the value of hard work and dedication.

Communication is the cornerstone of a positive and productive youth baseball experience. By fostering active listening, encouraging open dialogue, addressing concerns constructively, and role modeling positive interactions, coaches and parents can create an environment where young athletes feel valued, understood, and motivated. This approach not only enhances the players' experience but also contributes to their personal and athletic development, laying the groundwork for lifelong skills both on and off the diamond.

5.3 MOTIVATING YOUNG ATHLETES: TIPS AND TECHNIQUES

Motivating young athletes in youth sports is like nurturing a garden. It requires patience, understanding, and the right environment to help each individual flourish. The motivation that drives each player can vary significantly, and recognizing the difference between intrinsic and extrinsic motivation is the first step in cultivating a thriving team.

Understanding Motivation in Youth Sports

Motivation acts as the engine that propels young athletes towards their goals, and it comes in two main forms:

- Intrinsic Motivation: This springs from within the athlete. It's the joy of hitting a ball, the satisfaction of mastering a new pitch, or the thrill of competition. It's about the love of the game.

- Extrinsic Motivation: This comes from external rewards. It could be trophies, medals, praise from coaches and parents, or even the promise of post-game treats. While it can be effective in the short term, it's intrinsic motivation that often leads to long-term commitment and enjoyment in sports.

Creating a blend of both types of motivation can be beneficial, but the aim is to foster a deeper, intrinsic love for the game that keeps players engaged even when external rewards are not present.

Setting Achievable Goals

Goals are the landmarks that guide young athletes on their sports journey. They provide direction and a sense of purpose. However, not just any goal will do. They need to be SMART:

- Specific: Clearly defined goals are more effective. "Improve batting accuracy" is more actionable than "be a better batter."
- Measurable: Quantifiable goals allow athletes to track their progress. "Hit 15 out of 20 pitches in the batting cage" is measurable.
- Attainable: Goals should stretch the athlete's abilities but remain within reach to avoid frustration.
- Relevant: Goals need to align with the athlete's interests and the sport's demands.

- Time-bound: Adding a timeframe creates a sense of urgency and helps in planning.

Guiding young players in setting and refining their goals not only fuels their motivation but also teaches valuable life skills in planning and perseverance.

Creating a Supportive Environment

The environment in which young athletes train and compete significantly impacts their motivation and development. A supportive environment is characterized by:

- Positive Reinforcement: Highlighting what athletes do well, rather than focusing solely on mistakes, builds confidence and encourages them to keep striving.
- Encouragement After Failure: Showing support and offering constructive feedback after setbacks teaches athletes that failure is not the end but a step towards improvement.
- Opportunities for Leadership: Allowing young players to take on leadership roles, even in small capacities, instills a sense of responsibility and boosts motivation.
- Emphasis on Effort Over Outcome: Praising effort and improvement, rather than just wins and losses, helps athletes focus on what they can control—their hard work and dedication.

Creating such an environment requires conscious effort from coaches, parents, and the athletes themselves. It's about crafting a culture that values growth, learning, and the sheer joy of participation.

Recognizing and Celebrating Progress

Acknowledgment and celebration of progress are vital in keeping young athletes motivated. Here are a few ideas:

- Progress Parties: Periodic team gatherings to celebrate achievements, big and small, can boost team spirit and individual motivation.

- Individual Recognition: Personalized feedback sessions where coaches highlight each player's growth since the start of the season can reinforce the value of their effort and dedication.

- Public Acknowledgment: Recognizing achievements during team meetings or through team communication channels makes athletes feel valued and seen by their peers and coaches.

- Goal-Tracking Charts: Visual representations of progress towards individual and team goals can be incredibly motivating. It's a tangible way for players to see how far they've come.

Celebrating progress isn't about grand gestures. It's the consistent, thoughtful acknowledgment of effort, improvement, and achievement that fuels athletes' drive to keep pushing forward.

In motivating young athletes, the aim is to spark that intrinsic drive to play, improve, and enjoy the sport for its own sake. It's about setting meaningful goals, creating an environment that nurtures growth and resilience, and recognizing every step forward. This approach doesn't just build better athletes; it helps shape confident, dedicated individuals ready to tackle challenges both on the field and in life.

5.4 HANDLING DISAPPOINTMENT AND ENCOURAGING RESILIENCE

In the landscape of youth baseball, the highs of victory often walk hand in hand with the lows of disappointment. The true test of a young athlete's character isn't in how they handle success, but in how they navigate the rough waters of setbacks. This section unfolds the playbook on guiding young players through disappointment, building their resilience, and fostering a mindset that views challenges as stepping stones to mastery.

Teaching Players to Handle Disappointment

Disappointment, when channeled correctly, can be a powerful motivator. Here are strategies to help young players turn setbacks into growth opportunities:

- Normalize Feelings of Disappointment: Start by acknowledging that feeling down after a loss or a personal setback is perfectly normal. Sharing stories of professional athletes who faced similar challenges emphasizes that even the best have their off days.

- Identify Learning Opportunities: Post-game discussions can be pivotal. Encourage players to identify what they learned from the experience. Maybe it was a tactical error that could be avoided next time, or perhaps it highlighted an area for skill development.

- Set Short-Term, Achievable Goals: After a setback, setting small, attainable goals can help players regain confidence. It might be as simple as focusing on a specific skill during practice or achieving a personal best in a drill.

Building Resilience

Resilience is the backbone of not just a successful athlete, but a thriving individual. Here's how to cultivate it in young players:

- Foster a Positive Team Environment: Celebrate effort and improvement as much as, if not more than, wins. This creates a team culture where players feel supported to take risks and push their limits without fear of failure.

- Encourage Self-Reflection: Prompt players to reflect on their responses to challenges. Did they give up, or did they dig deeper? Self-reflection helps them recognize their growth in resilience over time.

- Stress the Importance of Persistence: Use examples of athletes who succeeded through sheer persistence. Stories where players overcame obstacles by not giving up can inspire young athletes to keep going, even when the going gets tough.

Supporting Players Through Challenges

The role of coaches and parents in supporting young athletes through tough times cannot be overstated. Here are ways to ensure players feel backed up:

- Listen Actively: Sometimes, all a player needs is someone to listen to their frustrations without immediately offering solutions. Active listening shows that you value their feelings and perspectives.

- Offer Constructive Feedback: Feedback should focus on what the player can control—effort, attitude, and the willingness to learn. Avoid focusing on aspects beyond their control, like refereeing decisions or the weather.

- Be Available: Let players know you're there for them, not just as a coach or a parent but as someone who genuinely cares about their development, both on and off the field.

Fostering a Growth Mindset

At the heart of resilience lies a growth mindset—the belief that skills and abilities can be developed through dedication and hard work. Cultivating this mindset in young players can transform their approach to baseball and life:

- Emphasize Learning Over Winning: Shift the focus from winning games to learning and improving. This helps players understand that mistakes are not failures, but opportunities to get better.
- Celebrate Effort and Progress: Make a big deal out of personal bests, no matter how small. This reinforces the idea that effort leads to improvement, ingraining the principles of a growth mindset.
- Teach the Power of "Yet": The word "yet" can be incredibly empowering. A player might not be able to hit a curveball or master a pick-off move yet, but with practice and persistence, they will. This tiny word opens up a world of possibility and perseverance.

In navigating the journey of youth baseball, disappointment and setbacks are inevitable. Yet, within these challenges lie golden opportunities—to teach young players about resilience, to support them in their moments of doubt, and to instill a growth mindset that sees beyond temporary defeats to the vast potential for learning, improvement, and eventual success. Through these lessons, young athletes learn not just to be better players, but more importantly, to be resilient individuals ready to face life's challenges with determination and grace.

5.5 THE IMPORTANCE OF CROSS-TRAINING IN YOUTH SPORTS

In the dynamic world of youth baseball, the concept of cross-training emerges as a beacon of versatility and resilience. It's a training philosophy that encourages athletes to engage in diverse physical activities beyond the confines of their primary sport. This approach not only enriches the athletic journey but also lays the foundation for a more profound, well-rounded development.

Benefits of Cross-Training

Cross-training is not merely a supplement to baseball training; it's an integral component of a young athlete's growth. Its benefits extend across various dimensions:

- Injury Prevention: Diverse physical activities distribute the physical stress across different muscle groups, reducing the risk of overuse injuries common in specialized sports training.
- Improved Overall Athleticism: Engaging in multiple sports enhances general athletic abilities, such as agility, endurance, and strength, which are transferable and beneficial across all sports, including baseball.

- Reduced Burnout: The variety that comes with cross-training keeps the training regimen exciting and engaging, mitigating the monotony that can lead to burnout in young athletes.

Cross-Training Activities for Baseball Players

The selection of cross-training activities should complement the physical and mental demands of baseball, offering a refreshing yet constructive break from routine practice. Here are activities that harmonize with baseball's requirements:

- Swimming: This low-impact exercise is excellent for building cardiovascular endurance and muscular strength without straining the joints, offering a perfect recovery activity.
- Soccer: Playing soccer enhances footwork, agility, and cardiovascular fitness. The dynamic nature of the game also improves spatial awareness and teamwork skills.
- Yoga: Incorporating yoga into a young athlete's routine can significantly improve flexibility, balance, and core strength. Additionally, yoga practices support mental focus and stress management.

Integrating Cross-Training into Practice

The challenge lies in weaving these activities seamlessly into the existing training framework without overwhelming young athletes. Here are strategies to integrate cross-training effectively:

- Scheduled Cross-Training Days: Allocate specific days within the training calendar exclusively for cross-training activities. This ensures a structured approach, providing athletes with clear expectations and something to look forward to.

- Off-Season Focus: The off-season presents an opportune window for intensifying cross-training efforts. It's a period for recovery and building foundational skills that will benefit the athlete in the baseball season.

- Incorporate as Warm-Up or Cool-Down Routines: Begin or conclude regular practice sessions with short cross-training activities. For example, yoga stretches can serve as an excellent cool-down routine after intensive baseball practice.

Encouraging Multi-Sport Participation

The encouragement of multi-sport participation by parents and coaches plays a pivotal role in fostering a supportive environment for cross-training. Highlighting the long-term benefits of developing varied athletic skills and interests can motivate young athletes to explore and engage in multiple sports. Here's how to cultivate this encouragement:

- Highlight Successful Multi-Sport Athletes: Share stories of professional athletes who excelled in multiple sports during their youth. This not only serves as inspiration but also validates the benefits of a multi-sport background.

- Organize Multi-Sport Camps and Clinics: Collaborating with local sports clubs or schools to organize camps and clinics that offer exposure to various sports can ignite interest among young athletes to try new activities.

- Parent-Athlete-Coach Dialogues: Regular discussions among athletes, parents, and coaches about the athlete's interests, goals, and well-being can foster a supportive atmosphere. These dialogues can help in identifying the right balance and mix of sports that align with the athlete's aspirations and development needs.

Cross-training, with its multifaceted benefits, stands as a testament to the philosophy that specialization in youth sports should not come at the expense of overall physical, mental, and emotional development. By embracing diverse physical activities, young baseball players not only enhance their performance on the diamond but also embark on a more enriching athletic journey. This journey, characterized by varied experiences, broadened skills, and reduced burnout, prepares them not just for the next season but for a lifetime of healthy, active living.

Through strategic integration, encouragement of multi-sport participation, and thoughtful selection of complementary activities, coaches and parents can unlock the full potential of cross-training. It's an approach that transcends traditional training paradigms, offering young athletes a broader perspective on sports, an arsenal of transferable skills, and, most importantly, a sustained passion for physical activity. In this light, cross-training emerges not just as a training methodology but as a cornerstone of holistic athletic development, nurturing well-rounded, resilient, and versatile athletes ready to meet the dynamic demands of baseball and beyond.

5.6 ORGANIZING TEAM ACTIVITIES
THAT BUILD CAMARADERIE

In the heart of every team lies a bond that, when nurtured, can elevate them from a group of individuals to a unified force. The essence of building this bond, or camaraderie, lies in shared experiences that extend beyond the field. These moments forge trust, instill a sense of belonging, and celebrate the mosaic of personalities and backgrounds that make up the team. Here, we delve into the ways to cultivate these vital connections.

Importance of Team Bonding

The fabric of a team is woven from more than just practices and games; it's crafted through laughter, shared challenges, and collective triumphs. Team bonding activities foster an environment where players feel comfortable relying on each other, both in and out of play. This trust translates into better communication and understanding on the field, leading to a more cohesive unit. Moreover, a sense of belonging encourages players to express themselves openly, contributing their unique strengths towards the team's goals.

Ideas for Team-Building Activities

To strengthen team dynamics, consider these activities that blend fun with purpose:

- Team Outings: Schedule outings that offer a break from the routine. A day at a ropes course can mirror the trust and teamwork needed on the field, while a group hike emphasizes the journey and collective effort over individual achievement.

- Community Service Projects: Engaging in community service as a team not only fosters a sense of pride and accomplishment but also teaches players the value of giving back. Whether it's a cleanup day at a local park or volunteering at a food bank, these experiences can deepen the players' connections with each other and their community.

- Team Challenges: Organize challenges that require teamwork and strategic thinking, like a scavenger hunt or a team-based trivia night. These activities can spark friendly competition and encourage players to work together in new ways.

- Cooking Competitions: A cooking challenge, perhaps making the best team taco, can be a lighthearted way to promote teamwork. It encourages players to communicate, delegate tasks, and, of course, enjoy the fruits of their labor together.

Involving Players in Planning

For these activities to truly resonate, it's crucial to involve players in the planning process. This not only increases their excitement and engagement but also gives them a sense of ownership over the team culture. Start with a brainstorming session to gather ideas, and then form small committees to take charge of organizing different events. This approach encourages leadership and ensures that the activities reflect the interests and passions of the team.

Celebrating Team Diversity

Each team is a tapestry of diverse backgrounds, experiences, and personalities. Embracing and celebrating this diversity is key to building a strong, inclusive team culture. Here are some ways to honor the uniqueness of each player:

- Cultural Potluck: Host a potluck where players bring dishes that represent their cultural heritage. This not only makes for a delicious gathering but also opens conversations about different traditions and histories.
- "Get to Know You" Sessions: Dedicate time during team meetings for players to share about themselves, whether it's their hobbies, family traditions, or personal heroes. These sessions can reveal common interests and foster empathy among teammates.
- Diversity Workshops: Consider bringing in a speaker or organizing workshops that address topics like inclusivity and respect. Such educational opportunities can deepen players' understanding and appreciation of each other's differences.

Through these carefully crafted activities and initiatives, teams can transform into more than just a group of athletes; they become a community. A community where trust, inclusivity, and a shared sense of purpose drive them towards not only their goals on the field but also towards becoming empathetic and supportive individuals off it. In doing so, they set the foundation for a team culture that thrives on the collective strengths and unique contributions of each member, propelling them towards success in every endeavor they undertake together.

5.7 NURTURING A LOVE FOR THE GAME BEYOND WINNING

In the heart of every young baseball player beats a growing passion for the game—a passion that, when nurtured correctly, flourishes beyond the scoreboard's tale of wins and losses. This section explores the vibrant paths coaches and parents can tread to instill a lasting love for baseball in the hearts of young athletes.

Focusing on the Joy of Playing

The crack of the bat, the thrill of the catch, the rush of stealing a base—these are the moments that infuse baseball with joy. Highlighting these experiences during practice and games helps young players connect with the inherent fun of the sport. Here are a few ways to keep the spirit alive:

- Play for the Sake of Playing: Sometimes, let the kids play without the pressure of coaching or correcting. This free play allows them to experiment, be creative, and most importantly, have fun.
- Mix It Up: Introduce variations of baseball games, like Wiffle ball or kickball, during practice. These games still develop skills but in a less structured, more enjoyable way.
- Celebrate the Small Victories: Whether it's a well-executed play or an improvement in technique, celebrating these moments encourages a positive association with the game.

Teaching the History and Traditions of Baseball

Baseball is rich with traditions and history, and sharing these stories can deepen a young player's appreciation for the game. Consider:

- Storytime Sessions: Dedicate time to discuss legendary players, iconic games, and pivotal moments in baseball history. These tales of triumph and perseverance can be incredibly inspiring.

- Visit Historic Sites: If possible, organize trips to baseball museums or historic ballparks. Standing in places where legends played can be an awe-inspiring experience for young athletes.

- Incorporate Baseball Lore into Practice: Use stories from baseball history to teach lessons about sportsmanship, teamwork, and the importance of practice.

Encouraging Lifelong Participation

Fostering an environment where baseball is a lifelong journey rather than a short-term competition can significantly impact young players' attitudes towards the game. Here's how:

- Promote Multiple Roles: Teach players that one can enjoy baseball in many capacities—be it as a player, coach, umpire, or fan. This understanding can keep them connected to the game long after their playing days.

- Encourage Community Involvement: Get players involved in local baseball communities, whether through volunteering at events or attending local games. This involvement helps them see the value of the sport beyond personal achievement.

- Highlight the Health Benefits: Emphasize how playing baseball can contribute to a healthy lifestyle. Understanding these benefits can motivate players to stay involved in the sport.

Role of Parents and Coaches in Fostering Passion

The influence of parents and coaches in nurturing a young athlete's love for baseball cannot be overstated. Their enthusiasm, support, and approach to the game play a crucial role in shaping the player's perspective. Here are some ways they can contribute:

- Model Positive Behavior: Show excitement for the game, whether you're playing catch in the backyard or cheering from the stands. Your enthusiasm is contagious.
- Provide Opportunities for Growth: Encourage players to take on new challenges, whether it's trying out for a more competitive team or learning a new position. These opportunities can rekindle interest and passion in the game.
- Support Balanced Involvement: Ensure that baseball is a part of a well-rounded life. Encouraging academic pursuits, hobbies, and social activities alongside baseball can prevent burnout and keep the love for the game alive.
- Share Your Own Stories: Personal stories about your experiences with baseball can be incredibly motivating. Share why you love the game, memorable moments, and what baseball has taught you about life.

In weaving these threads of joy, history, lifelong participation, and supportive guidance, we create a tapestry that celebrates baseball in its purest form—not just as a sport but as a source of joy, lessons, and enduring passion. It's about creating an experience that young players carry with them, an experience that fuels not only their love for baseball but also their appreciation for the camaraderie, challenges, and triumphs that the game brings into their lives. In doing so, we ensure that their connection to baseball is not measured by the runs on the scoreboard but by the smiles on their faces, the fire in their hearts, and the memories they cherish—forever linking them to the beautiful game of baseball.

5.8 SAFETY PROTOCOLS EVERY COACH AND PARENT SHOULD KNOW

In the vibrant world of youth baseball, where every pitch, swing, and slide carries the promise of growth and excitement, the safety of our young players stands paramount. The diamond, while a place of joy, holds inherent risks that require our vigilant attention and proactive measures. This section sheds light on crucial safety protocols, ensuring that the game remains not only enjoyable but, above all, safe for every player stepping onto the field.

Understanding Safety Risks

The first step in safeguarding our players involves a clear understanding of the potential risks they face. From the minor scrapes and bruises that are almost rites of passage in the sport, to more concerning issues like concussions and overuse injuries, being aware of these hazards sets the foundation for effective prevention. It's this knowledge that empowers us to create a playing environment where risks are minimized, and the well-being of each child is the top priority.

- Overuse Injuries: Particularly prevalent in pitchers, these stem from repetitive motion and excessive strain on specific muscle groups.
- Impact Injuries: Whether from a ball, bat, or collision with another player or base, these sudden impacts can range from minor to severe.
- Heat-Related Illnesses: On sweltering summer days, the risk of heat exhaustion or heat stroke becomes an invisible opponent to be reckoned with.
- Concussions: Though less common than in contact sports, the potential for concussions exists, especially with errant pitches or base-running collisions.

Essential Safety Protocols

Armed with an understanding of these risks, we turn our focus to the protocols that serve as our primary defense against them. These guidelines are the pillars upon which a safe playing environment is built.

- Proper Use of Equipment: Ensuring players use helmets, gloves, and protective gear correctly can prevent many injuries. This includes the correct fitting of helmets and the use of heart guards for pitchers.

- Warm-Up Routines: Dynamic stretches and gradual warm-up exercises prepare the body for the physical demands of the game, reducing the likelihood of muscle strains and injuries.
- Pitch Count Limits: Adhering to pitch count guidelines helps prevent overuse injuries in young pitchers, allowing their arms the necessary rest between appearances.
- Immediate Response to Injuries: Establishing a clear protocol for responding to injuries—ranging from minor cuts to potential concussions—ensures that every incident is treated with the appropriate level of care.

Creating a Safety-First Culture

Beyond the implementation of protocols lies the cultivation of a culture that places safety at the forefront of every decision, every practice, and every game. This culture is not the responsibility of coaches alone but a shared commitment among players, parents, and the wider baseball community.

- Education and Awareness: Regular discussions and workshops on safety topics keep the importance of player well-being in the collective consciousness of the team and their supporters.
- Open Communication Channels: Encouraging players to speak up about pain, discomfort, or concerns they have regarding their well-being fosters an environment where issues can be addressed before they escalate.
- Lead by Example: Coaches and parents set the tone for a safety-first approach by consistently demonstrating

and reinforcing safe practices, both in how they conduct themselves and in their expectations for players.

Emergency Preparedness

Despite our best efforts to prevent them, emergencies can and do occur. Being prepared for these moments can make all the difference in the outcome. The key to effective emergency preparedness lies in planning, communication, and education.

- Emergency Action Plan (EAP): Having a well-documented EAP that is regularly reviewed with coaches, volunteers, and even players ensures that everyone knows their role in an emergency situation. This plan should include procedures for dealing with severe injuries, sudden illnesses, and other emergencies that could occur during practice or games.

- First Aid Training: Ensuring that all coaches and team volunteers have up-to-date first aid and CPR certification equips them with the knowledge to respond effectively to injuries and health issues.

- Emergency Contacts and Medical Information: Keeping a readily accessible list of emergency contact numbers and pertinent medical information for all players allows for swift action when time is critical.

- First Aid Kits: Maintaining well-stocked first aid kits at all practices and games, and ensuring that they are easily accessible, is a simple yet crucial step in emergency preparedness.

In the heart of youth baseball lies a commitment—not just to the sport and its cherished traditions but to the young athletes who bring it to life. This commitment extends beyond teaching the rules of the game or fostering athletic prowess; it encompasses a dedication to the health, safety, and well-being of every player. By understanding the safety risks unique to baseball, adhering to essential safety protocols, nurturing a culture that prioritizes safety above all, and preparing for emergencies with foresight and diligence, we honor this commitment. We ensure that the game remains a source of joy, growth, and fond memories for our young players, safeguarding not only their physical health but the spirit of baseball itself.

5.9 DEVELOPING LIFE SKILLS THROUGH BASEBALL

Baseball, much like a complex puzzle, presents players with a variety of challenges and opportunities for growth. It's in navigating these moments that young athletes pick up invaluable life skills, extending the game's influence far beyond the diamond. This section shines a light on how the principles of baseball can serve as a powerful tool for teaching teamwork, leadership, time management, and problem-solving.

Teaching life skills through baseball starts on the field but resonates in every aspect of a player's life, offering lessons that shape their approach to challenges, goals, and teamwork. These skills, once cultivated, stay with the players, guiding them through various life situations.

Integrating Life Skills into Coaching

The essence of coaching transcends teaching technical skills; it involves preparing young athletes for life. Here are ways to weave life lessons into baseball coaching:

- Teamwork and Collaboration: Highlight how every play, from a double play to a relay throw, requires trust and cooperation among teammates, mirroring the importance of collaboration in life.
- Leadership Opportunities: Rotate team captaincy or assign players different leadership roles during practices and games, allowing them to experience leadership firsthand. This not only boosts their confidence but also teaches responsibility.
- Time Management: Encourage players to balance baseball, academics, and personal time, reflecting the real-life juggle of responsibilities. Discuss strategies during team meetings, offering a platform for players to share tips and insights.
- Problem-Solving: Use game scenarios to enhance players' problem-solving abilities. Pose hypothetical situations and prompt players to strategize solutions, fostering analytical thinking that's applicable beyond the game.

Role Modeling and Mentorship

The impact of a coach or parent's actions often speaks louder than their words. Here's how to be an effective role model and mentor:

- Exemplify Positive Behavior: Display the qualities you wish to instill. Show respect, perseverance, and sportsmanship at all times, demonstrating that these values matter both on and off the field.
- Open Dialogue: Maintain open channels of communication. Share your own experiences, including setbacks and how you overcame them, to build a connection and offer guidance.
- Encourage Initiative: Praise players for taking initiative, whether it's helping set up equipment, leading a warm-up, or supporting a teammate. Recognizing these actions reinforces the value of taking charge and contributing to the team.

Encouraging Reflection and Personal Growth

Reflection is a powerful tool for personal development. It allows players to acknowledge their growth, understand their experiences, and apply their learning to other life areas. Here are some strategies to encourage this reflective process:

- Post-Game Reflections: After games, have a brief team reflection session. Discuss what was learned, what could be improved, and how the experience contributes to personal growth.
- Individual Journals: Encourage players to keep a journal of their baseball experiences, focusing on what they learned about teamwork, leadership, and facing challenges. This habit of self-reflection fosters a deeper understanding of their growth journey.

- Goal Setting and Review Sessions: Regularly set aside time to set personal and team goals, then review these goals periodically. This not only enhances their focus and motivation but also teaches the importance of setting, pursuing, and achieving objectives.

Through baseball, young athletes learn to navigate life's pitches, whether they come straight down the middle or curve unexpectedly. The game becomes a classroom where lessons in teamwork, leadership, time management, and problem-solving prepare them for the varied challenges of life. Coaches and parents play pivotal roles in this educational process, serving as mentors who guide, support, and inspire.

By integrating life skills into coaching, exemplifying these virtues, encouraging reflection, and fostering personal growth, we offer young players a toolkit for success that extends far beyond the baseball field. It's in these lessons, learned between bases and beyond games, that the true value of youth baseball is realized.

As we close this chapter, we're reminded that baseball is more than just a sport; it's a medium through which young players learn, grow, and prepare for the vast world outside the diamond. The skills they develop, the lessons they learn, and the growth they experience enrich their lives, equipping them to step confidently into whatever role or challenge they may face next.

CONCLUSION

As we draw the curtains on this comprehensive journey through the vibrant world of youth baseball, it's essential to reflect on the ground we've covered together. From the early pages, where we delved into the rich history and fundamental rules of baseball, to the advanced strategies that shape the game's competitive edge, this book has been a roadmap from novice beginnings to a place of deeper understanding and skill.

Through these chapters, we've navigated the transformation that comes with dedication to the game—a shift from grappling with basic terms and selecting the right equipment to mastering nuanced batting techniques, strategic pitching, and dynamic fielding. More than that, we've explored the mental fortitude required to excel, the leadership that inspires teams, and the pivotal role that you, as parents and coaches, play in nurturing young talent.

We've dissected the essential components of starting strong with foundational skills, underscored the dual pillars of mental and physical strength, ventured into the realm of advanced tactics, and recognized the irreplaceable influence of supportive mentors in a player's journey. For the young players who've accompanied us, remember, the essence of your growth lies in consistent practice, unyielding perseverance, and the resilience to bounce back stronger from setbacks. Parents, your unwavering support, balanced encouragement, and keen understanding make the world of difference, creating an environment where young athletes thrive. And to the coaches, your insight into effective teaching, your ability to motivate and your knack for fostering team unity are the backbone of any successful team.

But beyond techniques and tactics, we've embraced a holistic approach to baseball, acknowledging that true success in this game transcends physical prowess. It's about mental toughness, emotional intelligence, and the strength found in a community that rallies together. This synergy of body, mind, and spirit is what molds not just great players, but great individuals.

Now, the ball is in your court. I encourage you to take the lessons gleaned from these pages and weave them into your practice, your coaching strategies, and your support systems. Approach every game, every practice, with a heart full of enthusiasm, an eagerness to learn, and a steadfast commitment to personal and collective growth.

Share your journey with others. Let the stories of how these lessons have transformed your approach to baseball, or that of your young athlete, serve as a beacon for others walking this path. In doing so, we can foster a community of learners, enthusiasts, and champions, bound by our love for the game and our dedication to excellence.

In closing, let this book not just be a guide but a starting point. The journey of youth baseball, with all its joys, challenges, and triumphs, is a testament to the power of passion, dedication, and continuous improvement. May you carry forward this spirit, nurturing not just talent but a lifelong love for the game. Here's to the countless innings ahead, filled with growth, learning, and the pure delight of playing baseball. Let's play ball!

REFERENCES

- *Baseball: A Timeline* https://www.pbs.org/kenburns/baseball/timeline
- *Benefits of Sports for Adolescents* https://www.muhealth.org/conditions-treatments/pediatrics/adolescent-medicine/benefits-of-sports
- *Baseball Equipment List: Essential Baseball Gear Checklist* https://www.baseballmonkey.com/learn/youth-baseball-equipment-guide
- *How to Teach Sportsmanship in Youth Sports | Jersey Watch* https://www.jerseywatch.com/blog/how-to-teach-sportsmanship-in-youth-sports
- *Youth Baseball Coaching Tips for a Successful Season* https://traceup.com/8-tips-for-youth-baseball-coaches
- *How to Develop Throwing in Youth Baseball Players - GSP* https://www.gaynorstrength-pitching.com/blog/youththrowing
- *10 Best Baseball Hitting Drills for Kids - MOJO Sports* https://mojo.sport/coachs-corner/10-best-baseball-hitting-drills-for-kids/

- *Dartfish | Video Analysis Solutions to Improve Teams' and Athletes' Performance* https://www.dartfish.com/
- *Develop Mental Toughness in Young Athletes* https://www.successstartswithin.com/blog/how-do-young-athletes-develop-mental-toughness
- *5 Tips for Overcoming Sports Performance Anxiety in Student Athletes* https://www.hopkinsmedicine.org/health/wellness-and-prevention/5-tips-for-overcoming-sports-performance-anxiety-in-student-athletes
- *How Imagery and Visualization Can Improve Athletic ...* https://www.verywellfit.com/visualization-techniques-for-athletes-3119438
- *Sport nutrition for young athletes - PMC* https://www.ncbi.nlm.nih.gov/pmc/articles/PMC3805623/
- *7 Absolutes of How to Hit a Baseball* https://probaseballinsider.com/7-absolutes-how-hit-baseball/
- *Youth Baseball Pitching Mechanics: A Systematic Review* https://www.ncbi.nlm.nih.gov/pmc/articles/PMC5857730/
- *Pitcher-Catcher Communication Tips in Baseball* https://www.korebaseball.com/blogs/blog/enhancing-pitcher-catcher-communication-in-baseball-insights-and-strategies-for-optimal-performance
- *Mental Toughness Training for Athletes* https://www.peaksports.com/sports-psychology-blog/mental-toughness-training-athletes/
- *Planning an Effective Practice By Bill and Cal Ripken* https://www.baberuthleague.org/media/9327/CCMARCH2013.pdf

- *8 Essential Communication Tips for Youth Sports Coaches* https://www.teamsnap.com/blog/general-sports/8-essential-communication-tips-for-youth-sports-coaches
- *Motivating Young Athletes* https://appliedsportpsych.org/resources/resources-for-coaches/motivating-young-athletes/
- *Can Cross-Training Reduce Injuries in Young Athletes?* https://www.profysionj.com/blog/2021/october/can-cross-training-reduce-injuries-in-young-athl/

Dear Reader!

Thank You for Picking Up The Youth Baseball Handbook!

I'm truly grateful you chose this guide to support your baseball journey. Your engagement means the world to us and helps young players and their supporters find the resources they need to excel.

Why Your Review Is Invaluable:

- **Boost Visibility**: Your review helps others discover this book on Amazon.
- **Share Insights:** Offer insight to potential readers about the book's impact.
- **Build Community**: Connect with others in the baseball community.

Leaving a Review Is Simple:

- Visit The Youth Baseball Handbook on Amazon.
- Click "Write a customer review."
- Share your thoughts and experiences.

Every review, big or small, contributes significantly. Thank you for your support and for being a vital part of the baseball community.

Sincerely,

Pete Srodoski
Publisher, Pathways Press

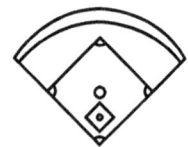